# WHITE LIMO

T0284271

# White Limozeen

## Steacy Easton

BLOOMSBURY ACADEMIC
NEW YORK • LONDON • OXFORD • NEW DELHI • SYDNEY

BLOOMSBURY ACADEMIC
Bloomsbury Publishing Inc
1385 Broadway, New York, NY 10018, USA
50 Bedford Square, London, WC1B 3DP, UK
29 Earlsfort Terrace, Dublin 2, Ireland

BLOOMSBURY, BLOOMSBURY ACADEMIC and the Diana logo are
trademarks of Bloomsbury Publishing Plc

First published in the United States of America 2024

Bloomsbury Publishing Inc does not have any control over, or responsibility
for, any third-party websites referred to or in this book. All internet
addresses given in this book were correct at the time of going to press.
The author and publisher regret any inconvenience caused if addresses
have changed or sites have ceased to exist, but can accept
no responsibility for any such changes.

Whilst every effort has been made to locate copyright holders the publishers
would be grateful to hear from any person(s) not here acknowledged.

A catalog record for this book is available from the Library of Congress.

ISBN: PB: 978-1-5013-9040-1
     ePDF: 978-1-5013-9042-5
     eBook: 978-1-5013-9041-8

Series: 33 1/3

Typeset by Deanta Global Publishing Services, Chennai, India
Printed and bound in Great Britain

To find out more about our authors and books visit www.bloomsbury.com
and sign up for our newsletters.

# Contents

# Introduction

Dolly Parton might be the most successful popular musician in America in the second half of the twentieth century—she sells well, she is beloved, she is rightfully known as a philanthropist. She embodies the kind of success story that the country likes to tell of itself—a rags to riches success who never forgot her roots, a good-times vulgarian who revels in bad taste. She has been all things for all people, and she is rewarded significantly for it. This universality took an epic amount of labor, and I would argue it was a result of deliberate recalculation after the 1980s. In the late 1980s, her career looked shattered, her 1986 album *Rainbow* was a disaster, her movie career ended ignobly with the Stallone vehicle *Rhinestone*, and she had a series of health concerns which resulted in canceling several concerts.

This book is about the album after *Rainbow*, about the recovery of Dolly's career after that singular disaster, but by extension, it's about what it took to get her there, about how calculated she was, how the success relied on stereotypes about gender, sexuality, class, and desire, about making the unreal real, about her high femme spirit, and about critiquing not only the album but some of the choices she has made. Dolly is not sacrosanct, and I hope the book isn't either.

It's difficult to write about Dolly because she is so well loved, and that adoration makes it difficult to render a full and complex picture. How do you write anything but a hagiography for someone who has won every award and entered every hall of fame possible? According to Chet Flippo, Parton joined the Nashville Songwriters Hall of Fame in 1986 and the larger Songwriters Hall of Fame in 2001. The Recording Academy honored her with a Lifetime Achievement Award in 2011. She has also won thirteen ACMs, ten Grammys, and nine CMAs as of April 2022. In December 2022, she became a member of the Rock and Roll Hall of Fame. Flippo doesn't even mention her three-time nomination for the Presidential Medal of Freedom or her nomination, under George W. Bush, for the Congressional Medal of Honor.

In an interview on *The Today Show* in February 2021, Parton talked about the Presidential Medal of Freedom, suggesting the caginess of her strategy (if it's not caginess, it's an unwillingness to be used by any one person for any one agenda). Parton says, "I couldn't accept [the award] because my husband was ill, and then they asked me again about it, and I wouldn't travel because of the COVID." Now, she continues, "I feel like if I take it, I'll be doing politics. So I'm not sure." The most telling moment in the interview is her refusal to own up to playing politics—like taking a medal under George W. Bush wasn't political, like being a working-class woman isn't essentially political, like negotiating Nashville wasn't political. Not being political is a notion that Dolly slips into when it is convenient for her to do so.

This slipperiness is typical of Dolly—if she wanted the medal, she could have had it mailed to her. There are legitimate concerns. There was the hint of not wanting to have the medal if Trump gave it to her; Dolly didn't speak out against Trump, and she didn't really endorse Trump either. To her credit, she was not like Loretta Lynn, who actively supported him, or Charlie Daniels, who would tweet every morning for years, asking about Benghazi, a conspiracy theory too complex to explain here.

On NPR, they quote from an appearance that Obama made on Stephen Colbert, where he says that he regretted not giving her a medal and that he was convinced that she had already gotten one. It's a curious notion, partially because the awarding of the medal is done by bureaucrats, and the information would have been available to Obama. Maybe he was thinking about the arts medal.

I wonder whether letting people view Dolly through the lens of achievement, or other oversimplified forms, protects her from questions of where the money goes, how the money comes in, about where exactly she is from, or who exactly she is. Dolly wants us to think of her as just a simple girl from the country, or a hillbilly, or an old-school broad, in the same way that she wants us to think of her as a sophisticated urbanite, or a successful businessperson. She works hard at making us think of her as just simple and incapable of being as calculating as she is.

Watching Dolly's career to the rest of the world mirrors the rest of that passage. The town might also be less cut off than Dolly's writing—she was born outside of the town of Sevierville, Tennessee, near a place called Locust Ridge, a more geographical feature then town. Sevierville itself was a mark for tourists from the 1910s onward—starting with the Great Smoky Mountain Railroads, and then from 1934 onward, the center of Great Smoky Mountain National Park and its resulting highway. The idea of Tennessee as remote was good for attendance numbers for that park, its scenic quality, and a kind of constructed yet easily accessible wilderness.

Dolly's fandom could be thought to be equally accessible—her queer fans think that a lifelong friendship with Judy Ogle means she may be queer, and her MAGA fans think that she may be MAGA. They collect evidence, they cite that evidence like scripture, and they are disappointed when that evidence is inconclusive. It must be said that she has voiced the most anemic support for Black Lives Matter at the height of the movement, not giving money publicly or attending rallies, in the same way that she will accept the love associated with being a queer icon while also waiting years to make official statements against the anti-trans legislation in her native Tennessee.

It might be useful here to strip away the actual persona.

Dolly is the daughter of Avie Lee Owens and Robert Lee Parton. Her father was a sharecropper. Her mother was a homemaker. Dolly grew up in Locust Ridge, in the Great Smoky Mountains in Tennessee. She is the seventh generation of her family who were born, raised, and died in that region. She had eleven siblings: Willadeene, David Wilburn, Coy Denver, Robert Lee, Stella Mae, Cassie Nan, Randel "Randy" Huston, Larry Gerald, Estel Floyd, Freida Estelle, and Rachel Ann.

Stella, the sixth of the twelve, is the only other sibling who has a substantial recording career. She sang in the church choir, in family circles, and in small churches and halls throughout East Tennessee. In her early twenties, she and her sisters Willadeene and Cassie, along with her mother, were in a gospel band. They also did regional commercials, mostly for cars. Stella's subsequent career somewhat resembled Dolly's—a national record deal with Elektra after that gospel run, a handful of chart hits, some regional theater, a guest role or two on *Dukes of Hazzard*, then a string of albums from smaller and smaller labels. It's a good life, and more of a career than most singers from her region would have had. There are dozens of singers from Appalachia who recorded an album or two for small regional labels, who almost made it to Nashville, but never got past home. Stella's skills were just good enough to be in one of those positions, but I cannot see her exceeding that without sharing Dolly's name.

She certainly had more of a musical career than her youngest sister, Rachel, who played Dolly on an ill-fated sitcom, *9 to 5*, or her brother Randy Parton, who used his connections to engage in some shady business with a dinner theater in the Carolinas. All of their careers, even Stella's, were gifts from Dolly, examples of her beneficence. Dolly made phone calls to labels and producers. She gave them money to start clubs and casinos. Dollywood included the Parton family in musical revues, keeping them constantly employed. She takes care of her own.

It is not impossible to imagine that Dolly could have gone in this more humble direction. Parton married her husband,

Carl Dean, when he was twenty-four and she was twenty. He has never worked in music but has always worked in trucking (driving them or organizing their driving) in a way that Parton has kept fairly discreet. She doesn't have any children, which might have been a career choice or of medical consequence; she has spoken in interviews about endometriosis, the condition resulting in a partial hysterectomy in 1982 that forced her to cancel some concert dates.

As of 2023, Dolly has been recording for sixty-six years, her first single being "Puppy Love" in 1957. Her early career was heavily managed by Porter Wagoner, and between 1967 and 1975, she appeared on 218 episodes of his television show before quitting to go off on her own. She claims that her signature song, "I Will Always Love You," is about Wagoner, and she has never spoken poorly of him, despite his reputation of being a difficult person to work with, especially for young women.

According to the Dolly Discography, to date, Dolly has recorded fifty-two studio albums and nine live albums, plus multiple "best ofs" and compilations. Twenty-one of those albums have gone gold or platinum, and forty-two have charted. She has had twenty-five number-one songs on the *Billboard* country charts and over three billion streams. She is responsible for a dozen of the defining songs of the American songbook, including "Jolene," "I Will Always Love You," "Down from Dover," "9 to 5," "Two Doors Down," "Why'd You Come in Here Lookin' Like That" and many others.

There is nothing else that Parton could have done. She is deeply successful within her own genre, noting where her career could have gone and directing it there. She has written about selling out, but she prefers the term "selling in," uniting audiences from a wide variety of genres, geographies, classes, and races and suiting her work, as well as a very specific idea of herself, to them. In a more cynical mode, it could be marketing; in a less cynical mode, it could be an extension of her own hospitality growing up.

There is something about how ingratiating she is to the rest of the country—and as an ambassador for her gender, for her genre, for her region, perhaps the world. Parton's status as an icon—as the subject of a Warhol painting, as someone who appeared on dozens of episodes of Johnny Carson, and then Letterman, who has gone viral in the last decade for singing at tiny Irish pubs and on the stages of Glastonbury, the biggest musical festival in the world—fails to reveal who Dolly herself is.

There is Dolly the person, who grew up in that little town in Tennessee, and Dolly the savvy businessperson, and Dolly the pop/country superstar. She didn't even grow up in Sevierville, which was the nearest small town. She didn't even grow up in Locust Ridge, which was the nearest geological place name near Sevierville. She grew up in a cabin, in a mountain lot that is inevitably called nestled, in the East Great Smoky Mountains, a range at the Southern end of the Appalachians.

In interviews and in her autobiography, she noted that her family home didn't have electricity or plumbing until she was in high school. She could trace her family's residency in those mountains back hundreds of years—her family tree could be traced to at least the Civil War.[1] This Appalachian heritage was one of the facts that Dolly and her audience mutually mythologized, turning the woman Dolly into the icon Dolly. An icon requires seamlessness, and so all of the stories that are told about Dolly must work toward a single goal—a goal which works against aesthetic or moral complexity to emerge. This is especially true of the American concept of fame, which excludes those who are too weird or too inaccessible. One way to recover some of the complexity is not to think of Parton's life as a straight trajectory out of Tennessee but to note the recalculations across her career. The successes may look linear, but the failures give us context, the most significant being *Rainbow*, her twenty-seventh studio album from 1987, and *White Limozeen*, from 1989. This book is about the latter, but the former provides context which cannot be underestimated.

Parton spent her entire life figuring out how to fit her small-town Appalachian life into a national or global context, to balance never leaving the holler and being as big of a star

---

[1] There are a number of people on the web who obsessively search for celebrities' family trees, and there are other people on the web who obsessively re-enact the Civil War, sometimes digitally and sometimes in person. There is a distant relative who was a volunteer in the Union army by the name of Benjamin Chrisman Parton. I will leave it as an exercise for the reader to figure out the politics of that. In private correspondence, the country music scholar Joseph Thompson notes that "East Tennessee, especially in the mountains, was heavily unionist during the civil war. It was also heavily Republican after the war . . . (Dolly) is white and southern, which comes with a series of assumptions, yet her actual family history undercuts those assumptions."

as possible, not only for Nashville—her ambition was more wide-ranging than that. Until *Rainbow*, she had gone from success to success, from singing at small stages throughout rural Tennessee to the regional fame of Porter Wagoner's television, to the chart successes and American Country Music awards, to the breakthrough singles of the late 1970s. There was a lot of sweat, hard work, and self-directed choices.

Parton was ruthless about being famous, and the ruthlessness centered and drove her career. From the regional success, she became a national and international success. It must be understood that the translation from regional to national success—from the honky tonk to Hollywood back lots—relied on abstracting the historical facts of Dolly's life into a hot ticket commodity. In those moments, Dolly did not become one woman from the holler or even a representative of genre like Loretta Lynn or Tammy Wynette. Instead, she slid into a larger American myth, if not several at the same time.

She became an example of the blonde who played dumb but was the smartest person in the room (see Mae West, Jean Harlow, or even Marilyn). She was the hillbilly or the redneck who city folks thought was backward but still won everything despite them. There is a cluster of American myths where the rural figure bests the urban sophisticate by verbal quickness—the sophisticate underestimates how smart the rural figure is and becomes entrapped in their own cleverness. Mark Twain does it all the time, from episodes where Tom Sawyer convinces other kids to do his work for him or when Huckleberry Finn outsmarts the thieves in the funeral incident. It continues into the twentieth century—

how Jed of the Beverly Hillbillies operates in that monied world, for example, or how Daisy Mae, invented by Al Capp to mock Appalachian people, is used as an example of their own resilience. It also returns back to the oral tradition in the hundreds of jokes made about the farmer's daughter and the traveling salesmen.[2]

The farmer's daughter joke has a pretty simple premise. A salesman is traveling through a rural region, most likely the Midwest or the South, depending on what point you are trying to make. Often the joke has him driving a car that is deeply inappropriate for the set of circumstances—a bright red sports car, for example. The car breaks down, and the salesman is trapped in the middle of nowhere. He walks to the nearest farmhouse, where the farmer (often without a wife) tells the salesman that he can stay the night and go to the mechanic in the morning. However, the farmer has two beautiful daughters, and they must be left alone.

There are dozens of versions of this, meta versions and riffs on riffs. Sometimes a farmer's wife is included, sometimes there is one daughter or two daughters or three daughters, sometimes there is the frustration of sexuality, sometimes sex happens. Reading or hearing these stories, there is often a hint of misogyny, the idea that a woman is a fungible currency between men or that a woman's purity must be maintained at all costs. None of the subtext should be denied. However, there

---

[2]It must also be mentioned that the idea of rovers, or rounders, salesmen, and the like also includes minstrelsy, too complex to mention in this limited space—but there has been an explosion of resources since Eric Lott's *Love and Theft* in 1993, including Paul Beatty's anthology *Hokum*.

is another quality here: the idea that the farmer knows exactly what is going on and is willing to pull a fast one on the salesman, or the idea that the salesman is stupid and cannot understand how the rural world operates, creates the central subtext of the joke—a tradition of American humor from the beginning. There is a more slippery kind of subtext here, one where the daughters choose to have sex with the salesman or choose not to, depending on the convenience of the joke—but they choose, they make arguments for their own autonomy, unsettling the rurality of the farmer and the urbanity of the salesmen, a double subversion, one that centers their desires or their ambiguities. In the best versions of this joke, the farmer's daughters, with their wits and their bodies, win—they move from the farm and its expectations.

Dolly's public persona is an excellent example of this; at her best, she becomes both the blond who consents to the salesman and the person doing the selling, the hillbilly and the urban sophisticate, and perhaps the prey and the person being preyed upon.

Sort of like the Tex Avery cartoon from the 1930s—*Red Hot Riding Hood*, where Red Riding Hood replaces the woods with a phallic deco skyscraper, becoming a cabaret dancer for a tuxedoed wolf. Parton, in all of her moods, can be the salesman, the farmer, the daughter, the cabaret dancer, and the wolf. Thus, she was the poor white trash extruded into pure product and the pious church girl who provided an example of American fortune or providence. She was the central, complex figure of country music—what could be described as both Saturday night and Sunday morning, collapsed into a singular figure.

In foregrounding Parton's Appalachian identity (and for Dolly, this is a white one, and as we will see, this whiteness has worked in concert with creators who imposed an Appalachian identity from the outside), it needs to be acknowledged that the first people of the region that Dolly Parton was from, which is often considered the "heart of Appalachia," were Cherokee. In fact, the whiteness of Appalachian in popular imagination connects to the idea that indigeneity around the same time was mostly western or southwestern. Andrew Jackson, signing the Indian Removal Act of 1830, forcibly marched the Cherokee[3] from near where Dolly Parton grew up, what was understood as Appalachia, to regions in the newly "Americanized" West—especially Oklahoma. The reason why so many people claim Cherokee heritage is the centrality of erasure of Cherokee peoples—the paperwork was bad, no one was there to dispute them, and so even Dolly could be caught saying things like, in *Hot Press*, in 2002:

> It was an illegitimate thing, so I mean it's not really in our genealogy. But my grandfather had told us many years ago—because my mother's people are very dark and we were always going, "Where'd this come from? We're Irish, English and Scottish!" Well, there was the girl that the grandpa loved, and all that, who was Cherokee indian. So anyway, somewhere down the road we've got some Cherokee—but mostly we're Irish. My father's people

[3]https://slate.com/news-and-politics/2015/10/cherokee-blood-why-do-so -many-americans-believe-they-have-cherokee-ancestry.html

were Irish-Scottish and my mother's people were English-American, so we're a real mixture of everything.[4]

This romanticizing of being born on the wrong side of the blanket, of mysterious heritage, and for claiming identity that might not be here, is quickly pulled back, and the Irish/English is recentered—Dolly's identity rests on which stories sound authentic, as much as what might be accurate.[5]

Before delving into what Dolly might have meant about being Appalachian, it might be useful to identify what exactly Appalachia is. At its simplest, it is viewed as resident of the Appalachian mountains, but I doubt when people say Appalachia, they mean Georgia or Alabama, where the range originates, or Maine, where the terminus of the Appalachian Trail is. I also doubt, unless there is a deliberate political claiming, that outside of the region people consider Appalachia as anything but white, though Dolly obviously did. I think that when most people talk about Appalachia, they are talking about a region of Kentucky, Tennessee, and some other neighboring states—which is viewed as remote; a land of moonshine, superstition, and centuries-long tradition; and more explicitly a land that modernism evaded. There is an assumption, in historian Appalachians, of a culture with strong kinship networks, who do not perform in public. Dolly's commitment to perform her regional identity on international stages mashes up the exterior view of the

[4]https://www.lmc.edu/about/news-center/articles/2022/feature-article4.htm
[5]https://www.hotpress.com/culture/happy-birthday-dolly-parton-revisiting-2002-interview-hot-press-22764685

region with the region's interior view, bringing something more iconic to the surface.

In 1979, anthropologist Allen Batteau, working through oral histories of Kentucky, made a few observations. He noted that in the oral histories of people from Appalachia, there was not one clear definition. He then noticed that when asked questions by outsiders, there would be long pauses and then complex answers. He asked an old timer if he ever lived up North, and the old timer waited, said no, and then said he worked in Gary, Indiana, for a few years. Working in Gary did not mean living in Gary; in similar ways to Dolly working in Los Angeles or New York, he also noticed how deeply the kinship networks were saying: A basic feature of Appalachian culture is the distinction between relationships based on proximity (neighborliness) and relationships based on kinship, and great value is attached to each. He talks about how family groups would not sit apart, except for church, where everyone was brothers and sisters in Christ. Realizing the ambivalence of definitions, Dolly's strong kin network has always been part of how she sold her music. She made everyone feel like they were regionally connected, but she also maintained a strict private life. Dolly knew how to mark the edges of a family, with the privacy about her husband and small inner circles, for example her friend Judy Vogel or later with her circle around Gallin; and she knew that there was a Southern solidarity, a slightly larger circle, and then the larger, superstar public—the networks were purposefully self-contained. This interiority made public was deliberate and also rested on figures which were on the edges of the place she grew up—namely sex workers. It was safer for

Dolly to perform at being a sex worker, a kind of aesthetic abstraction solidified with money, than it was for people who sold sex—and joking about them in the national media and rarely making work about them, there is a mark of separation from her kin, which makes jokes like that plausible.

The throughline of Dolly's career is how to extend those kinship networks, or to put it plainly, how to grow an audience while still having that audience think that you are performing close to your hometown—that she had not reached above her raising. To be authentic. How she connects to an audience is to view how successfully she sells "working class" authenticity. This becomes transactional— the audience wants her to perform successfully, considers themselves part of her kinship network because of these sales, and then Dolly widens those networks, seeing the sales. This audience relationship has two parts—that this global superstar is one of them, and a willingness for that superstar to pretend to be still living in rural Tennessee, or more accurately, to be poor. She was poor, and so she knows poverty. She is no longer poor, so she knows that poverty can be escaped. There is an ambition that working-class people view as moral. She does not avoid her working-class roots, she is not poor or stuck up; but she knows well-off and well-connected people—so maybe her listeners could too. She is a deeply successful capitalist but gives away a large amount of her money, and has enough of an ego to build a monument to her own upbringing while living far away from it—but she comes back. The coming back to her roots is key here, and before the construction of Dollywood, her movement away from the South isolated that audience. *White Limozeen* was the album that tried to explain why she moved to California and why she was returning, an album she spent less press time on than the opening of Dollywood later in 1989—the Jerusalem of White Trash returning.

The problem of authenticity, then, is that Dolly is not more authentic because she is poor but because of a geographic memory, continuing an idea of Appalachia that was crafted by others.

The first people that Dolly sang to were her family. Throughout her career, she continued to talk about them as the first people to perform with her. Stella Parton had complex things to say about Dolly, claiming that she didn't get help from her. In fact, Dolly often asked her sister to change her name in auditions, saying that she didn't invite Stella to take part in her mid-1980s variety shows and wouldn't perform duets with her. Dolly keeps her business private, and though she helps out her family, the intermingling of family and her professional career, her public and her private life, is quite rare. Things became even more complicated in 2023 when Stella, who up to that point had center-right politics and had previously used Twitter to support women and work against the Trump Republican takeovers, tweeted a set of racist rants against neighbors. Dolly has never been racist, but returning back to a landscape which mostly voted for Trump, or never really leaving a family whose politics might not have been hers, makes things even slipperier.

Dolly's work about Appalachia is not only about class (though it is connected to the gulf between where she was and where she is) or conventional ideas of heterosexual family—these ideas must be understood as a construction of gender as well. The stories about the farmer, his daughters, and the salesman, or the jokes that Capp makes about the neighborhood, are not only questions about poverty but about other kinds of moral failures, other ideas of profligacy, and lack of self-control. Dolly's deeply controlled songs function as a resistance to these imposed ideas. The size of Parton's birth family and her repeated mention of siblings in press, though part of her extended memory, were thought to be poor or backward or charming. As the audience for the genre became more suburban, their families became smaller and less intergenerational. Conservatives, especially in the 1980s, believed that those who were poor were so because of the profligacy—this included personal and social spending. The performance of class and the performance of gender are made one in Dolly, and the question becomes one of public and private distinctions.

Academic and music critic Eric Weisbard wrote a book called *Top 40 Democracy: The Rival Mainstreams of American Music*, which includes a chapter on Dolly to which this book is deeply indebted. One of the arguments that Weisbard makes is about reception and audience—that how people listen to music matters more than, or as much as, what we think of genres, or even that genres are established via a social contract between the audience and the performer. Weisbard notes that a country's complex connections between land and authenticity mean that the relationship between genre and audience is especially vexed and policed. Weisbard writes adroitly on gender, and I think that this policing is especially egregious and that this call for authenticity is harsh when it comes to women. To be called fake, for a woman, means that her gender is not real and her music is not real—

when she fails to perform authenticity, it is the act of not only performing music falsely but also performing gender falsely. It's not that men cannot play these kinds of games or that men are not rewarded when they perform them well (see Johnny Cash), but that men face far fewer expectations or none at all.

Weisbard talks about this when he quotes Mary A. Bufwack and Robert K. Oermann of *Finding Her Voice*, who said that "Dolly Parton is the most famous, most universally beloved, and most widely respected woman who has ever emerged from country music."

Weisbard expands on exactly what this could mean:

> But she is also the best example, male or female, of how country—the genre of working- class and rural white southerners—reinvented itself. Too often viewed as conservative or betraying rural tradition, country became pop with a different accent, as determined a claiming of consumer America as anything in the rock and R&B-driven Top 40. Because it served commercial imperatives, the music confronted changing times with confidence and humor more than "lost cause" intransigence. (72)

Weisbard notes radio play and sales, and in this careful listening, he notes the intersections of genres. Parton's working-class history centers on anxiety about sales. She wants to sell because she wants to be known outside of Nashville. She expands past the genre and through the gatekeepers of the country. The breakthrough success of Parton was a move from one genre to another without the plausible deniability of an explicit split; ironically, Parton's biggest success rests on a self-awareness, being both simultaneously "country" and "not country," she is least successful when the equilibrium is disturbed.

There was the assumption that when Dolly signed with Columbia, for the records that would eventually be *Rainbow* and *White Limozeen*, the move from country to being genre-less was a completed task—that she had finally become larger than Nashville, not the both/and but beyond binaries and categories. But she stumbled severely; an audience was not willing to hear a Dolly record that didn't have some cultural history. In this way, *White Limozeen* was a deliberate construction away from the pop sound—not only in who she chose to work with or how the record sounded but in songs like the title track, whose storytelling featured both her rejecting Los Angeles and having her kinfolk come from the mountains to witness it.

Dolly wants to keep the genres open—her goal is to keep the gate open. The question of Dolly then becomes a question of stretching the audience without the original audience snapping. Ironically, the audience itself was stretching—who was a country audience that had grown outside of the narrow kinship networks, and the inner networks seemed to be closer to Dolly or the idea of performing Dolly. This real/unreal ambivalent quality had a distinct commercial aspect. This might be cynical, but Parton had to sell her identity to an audience that was quickly moving or changing—the idea of the purity of Appalachia to people who were moving to the suburbs of the Sunbelt, for example. This, her creation of Appalachia, connected explicitly to an idea of Appalachia, an idea which whitewashed the original residents of the region or romanticized them as a historical fact which had no current history.

For Parton, the mid-to-late 1980s were really messy. It was a clean-up year from the fights between outlaw country and countrypolitan, the soft and the hard of the 1970s, between the racism of the southern srategy, and fights about integration, versus the simultaneous emergence of a Black and Latinx sound, between the suburbs and the cities, between the cities and the rural country, about the growing exurbs, and about grinding poverty. It took a decade of 1970s country music to try to work out the consequences. Then the 1980s came, and the money was rolling in; the *Urban Cowboy* film with John Travolta gave birth to a movement, and country's commercial success in urban centers became its own existential crisis. The odd thing about *Rainbow* was that, for twenty years, Nashville had been arguing about what exactly country music was, in often rancorous ways. (Chris Molanphy, the chart critic and host of Slate's *Hit Parade* podcast, has an episode on Garth Brooks that has a good history of this commercial period).

I am nervous about calls for purity and am excited when country reflects the messy patterns of actual listening.

The country critic Amanda Martinez[6] makes the argument that country music, especially in the late 1970s and the Reaganite 1980s, was a racial backlash to the more complex and open early 1970s. She also argues that the shift of country or hillbilly music from mostly rural to almost

---

[6]Amanda Martinez, "Redneck Chic: Race and the Country Music Industry in the 1970s," *Journal of Popular Music Studies* 32, no. 2 (2020): 128–143.

entirely suburban was a more or less completed task by 1980, and the work after 1980 was politically or socially an attempt to make that transition invisible in some capacity. The argument was about the idea of place. Namely, that the obsession with rusticity or rurality casts the idea of those spaces as all-white spaces. White people listening to white music in white spaces thought that the purity of the form reified their whiteness—ideologically, geographically. Or to quote Martinez directly:

> At a time of such unease, white, urban Americans with middle incomes found refuge in the Southern imaginary and the signifiers of white rusticity, most notably found in a celebration of the white male Southern figure, the "redneck," and his musical counterpart, country music.

Thinking about Martinez, about money, and the problem of audience, Dolly must have known exactly what was happening to Nashville, recognizing that poverty read no longer as kitsch but as an inspirational movement that one could rise out of, a purity that was politically cleaner and more marketable. The work had been done and now one must find ways to hide the work. Dolly had always been very good at hiding her work, at taking exactly what was needed for the audience to buy a narrative, to pretend that the work never happened.

Dolly knows better than anyone—all of the joking, and the deliberateness of *White Limozeen*, the audacity of the clarity of its construction, matters almost more than the music itself. Some of the music is definitely worth joking, but even then, the album is a melange of cowrites, covers, reworkings, and reconstructions. For a work that is so ruthless about returning back home after a failure, it is still as artificial as *Rainbow*—still has the factory sheen, and is still about the big city as much as it is about small towns, marking an audience's demographic shift.

Thus, *White Limozeen* is not only an album but a tactic in an ongoing attempt to rework personae. It's an album which argues that the persona has never really shifted or changed, that she was always the girl from Tennessee. Just as the audience pretended that they had not moved up a social class or had moved into the suburbs, Dolly had to reflect that denial in order for the album to become successful.

Aside from the ongoing problem of Dolly floating over her work, of the meta-discourse overwhelming the actual text, of the idea of Parton winning over the actual life of Parton, which is a huge aside, the text of Dolly is always a combination of talk show appearances, stage patter, costume changes, ribald jokes, the odd film or television appearance, the theme park, and the personal appearances—of the relic or the idea of the body being as corporeal as the actual body, sitting down to the actual music, there is a moment, and I think that this occurs in most country music songs, where one realizes the Dolly one has fully integrated is one of songs and not albums. A Parton text is successful when the persona and the song function in tandem, the person and the persona work collectively as one. Both sides need to be visible, and thus in tense balance. This is often most successful over the period of a song or two. There are a few great songs on *White Limozeen* but not enough to make the entire album memorable. There might be something more interesting in a total collapse and something thrilling about a complete success, but the album is unsteady, and the balance might not be achieved.

The album was more successful than *Rainbow*. It spent more than two years on the country charts and peaked at number three. It was eventually certified gold. It included a handful of good songs—a cover of the Jesus People classic "He's Alive," a few songs about returning back to the land, a bluegrass reworking of an REO Speedwagon hit, a duet with Mac Davis. The songs were constructed to get her country audience back, and though one could argue that there is a solid country aesthetic here—Ricky Skaggs produced it, Bela Fleck played on it—there is something more complex and difficult: the melancholy of a rescue mission, the sense that she is learning to work again after what critics considered a roteness on her previous album, a desire to reconsider what her persona means in the act of creation, and perhaps a quiet moment of reflection after the burn-it-all-down 1980s. Dolly's success is one that builds on the intersection of music-making and persona-building; it is rare that her work shows the work being done to make those intersections smooth. There is power, though, in transparency and something intriguing about the (perhaps inadvertent) transparency.

# 1
# Returning to Some Kind of Country

*White Limozeen* returns to "country." Whatever country music is, it is about performing authenticity.

Parton is universally beloved for her authenticity, but she has fake hair, fake teeth, a new face, infamously fake tits, and has labored greatly to be thinner. A woman tattoos her body with flowers to cover the scars from those surgical procedures, but her costumes for stage and television cover everything from her ankle.[1] A woman might have conservative social positions, have spent fifty years married to the same man, but is notorious for her dirty jokes. At the 2023 ACM awards, she suggested that GOAT stood for "Garth Organized a Threesome" on stage; in 2018, Jimmy Fallon left the stage after she told him a risque joke, in interviews with queer actor Leslie Jordan, he claims that "she loved a dirty joke now and then"; and Lily Tomlin has said similar things, for talking about dressing up like the town

---

[1] https://jezebel.com/dolly-partons-boobs-and-arms-are-covered-in-secret-tatt-1574168202

hooker (she has said this on Rosie O Donnell, Jimmy Fallon, for Barbara Walters in 1978), for playing a madam in *Best Little Whorehouse*. Parton dedicates songs to loving above all else, but her greatest love song was written perhaps not for that husband but for her old boss, someone she refuses to shit talk to, even if he deserves it.[2]

Dolly Parton has spent so much time and effort making art about the abject poverty of her childhood, which is also a mess of contradictions—she does not forget her poverty, and she tries to make sure that other people do not have to live through it. She does not get involved in politics, this is a consistent ethos. Dolly will not speak out about the coal mines or Wal-Mart's decimating her homeland (in fact, in 2023, she lent her name to a "line of Dolly Parton party supplies"),[3] though she will perform a collection of pretty radical work songs as the soundtrack to a Hollywood farce about the workplace (especially the song "Deportees"). Also, Dollywood does not pay a living wage. Indeed reports the

---

[2] This is Porter Wagoner, https://www.tennessean.com/story/entertainment /music/2015/12/26/dolly-parton-remembers-writing-always-love-you /77762172/. Dolly was about to go out on her own, Wagoner was controlling her, and she wrote this powerhouse ballad about loyalty to assuage the wound. Dolly is too polite to talk about what directly happened, but in her memoir "My Life in Lyrics," she hints that he was taking credit for songs which he didn't write, or at least the disagreement was business. Elvis was interested in recording it, but she turned him down, which deepens the irony of it being the concluding track to Priscilla. Whitney Houston never asked for the rights.

[3] https://www.countryliving.com/entertaining/a44811965/dolly-parton -party-walmart/

salary range as "Average Dollywood hourly pay ranges from approximately $10.66 per hour for Operator to $22.00 per hour for Carpenter. The average Dollywood salary ranges from approximately $15,000 per year for Team Assistant to $120,000 per year for Director of Accounting." Which is, to be fair, at its lowest, three dollars more than the minimum wage. The living wage for a single adult with no children in Sevier County has been calculated at a little more than $15 an hour, and for someone with children and only one parent working, three times that. She has received some praise for building a tourist industry in the Great Smoky Mountains, though it projects an idealized view of class and race, and which, until five years ago, had a Dixie Stampede that showcased the Confederate flag.

Dolly has made very specific social choices, which seem inevitable. Looking carefully at how she has seamlessly presented the performance of authenticity is key to understanding Dolly, not the saint or the abstract figure but the complex person who does a good job at selling a persona, so one doesn't see the person.

If one was being ungenerous (and who would want to be ungenerous to Dolly?) she got out of the holler through sheer force of will and talent and then created a set of performances about that experience, making her ideas of Appalachia more or less miserable, depending on the audience's needs at the time. I am thinking about how charming the depictions of her hometown are in Dollywood, or the sweet stories she tells on talk shows or in concerts—the same stories, over decades, meant to placate an audience with the idea that life was not that bad, though it seemed quite perilous in that moment.

Parton's career throughout the 1970s was an argument about place. Her music was settled into ideas of Tennessee. A picture of the log cabin she grew up in was on the cover of *My Tennessee Mountain Home* from 1973—the front porch falling off and the ground in front of the place hard-packed dirt. There was also a cluster of remade murder ballads around that time—stories of children lost in the woods, of unfaithful lovers racing home to deliver a bastard child, only to lose the child, and tales of absolute abject poverty. There were ways she wrote songs too. "Jolene," with its chorus sounding akin to traditional ballads like "Lord Randall" or how "I Will Always Love You" borrowed shape from hymns. The slickness of the 1980s could have been a break, but that she brought her audience with her came from the memory of these "traditional" songs. *White Limozeen*'s strategy of restructuring her authenticity against the separation of her audience and repairing the failure of the authenticity in *Rainbow* opens up a critique of the practice itself. It's not that Dolly was inauthentic or authentic—perhaps not useful critical terms—but that Dolly and her audience agreed that she was authentic, despite many arguments that she wasn't, or at least agreed until the argument was no longer commercially useful. The creation of *White Limozeen* was a response to this failure by explicitly and carefully constructing meaning via the tropes of Appalachia; it was an attempt to return to the ideas of Appalachia.

The studio environment at Treasure Island in Nashville is different from that in the RCA Studios in Los Angeles because Nashville is where real country is made, and Los Angeles is where real country is corrupted (for example,

Jimmy Rodgers and Louis Armstrong recording in Los Angeles, or the Cosmic Country of Graham Parsons or The Byrds, or the revival of Dwight Yoakam, or how the myth of the cowboy was invented as much in Studio Lots as it was in Music Row).

At the same time, *White Limozeen* is a lush, densely produced, and studio-originated album—a sound which costs a lot of money. It also features a back-to-the-land song, a gospel rave-up, and a title track where Dolly calls herself a hillbilly. Here, she argues that poverty is how she codes authenticity and, by extension, is the ticket into the studio—that because she was poor, she could be authentic everywhere. To be less poor is to be at risk of having that "authenticity pass" fail. The social capital of Appalachian realness, where one's location or poverty read as purity, and whose reading of purity made aesthetic claims, was a sales pitch—one that traditionally allowed her to trespass between rurality and the cosmopolitan, it's harder to play at being poor when she shows up at Studio 54 on a white horse. However, in this moment, she liberates herself from Appalachia as something studied. In the interviews and press in 1989, the same date as *White Limozeen*, it is often about the opening of Dollywood, a theme park that she made about her life, a spectacle of the Appalachian poverty. Her return to Selvin, Tennessee, was a return to make a burlesque of the poverty of her childhood, just as the album was a burlesque of her career in Los Angeles—both an attempt to reverse a career downturn.

Dolly always played this burlesque. On *White Limozeen,* Parton talks about the Appalachian landscape in abstract terms—the green earth, or the purity of a country that she can return to against the glitz of the city. Critics often misread the games that Parton was playing, losing to her wit. On the title track of *White Limozeen*, Parton describes herself as Daisy Mae in Hollywood, reclaiming an image foisted on her eight years earlier in *Rolling Stone* by Stephen Holden: "Parton's power as a folk heroine derives from her native smartness and a radiant wholesomeness that reveals her Daisy Mae sexiness to be a good-humored ploy for attention . . . " Of course, "the power" lacks any autonomy on Parton's end, it seems an impossibility that Parton could make herself Daisy Mae or that she could be the self-directed protagonist of the farmer's daughter joke.

There are other instances of underestimation as well—in a July 1982 issue of *Ladies Home Journal*, Cliff Jahr circles the whole canon, comparing Dolly to "Mae West, Daisy Mae, Madame Du Berry, two Marilyn Monroes, and every mistress of ceremonies who ever worked in burlesque." Note the most obvious examples—the ones we have seen already, but also Du Berry, who was a mistress of the French King Louis XV, whose brother forged her birth certificate to disguise her age and poor origins, the odd doubling of Marilyn, and the even odder notion that Parton is not a burlesque dancer but the boss of burlesque dancers, someone who controls them. For Jahr, power through sex, and maybe a bit of dishonesty, is the key to Parton.

Daisy Mae was the blonde, buxom creation of Al Capp—a woman caught in the faux Appalachian town of DogPatch who eventually married Li'l Abner. Capp was a Jew who grew up in New Haven, Connecticut. His parents were from

Latvia. His father sought to be a cartoonist but ended up in a series of failed businesses instead. His sisters would also become cartoonists. His creation, *Li'l Abner*, an outsider's imagining of Appalachia, greatly influenced how America understood the region and its culture, despite the fact that Capp's idea of Appalachia reflected no real understanding of how the place and tradition existed.

Before Dolly, popular understandings of Appalachia were shaped by naughty jokes at the expense of women or the working class. Dolly took those dirty jokes and turned everything around, making a working class, hyper femme, refusal of what was expected of her. There was a more complicated narrative too. Appalachia was often thought of as a place of authenticity because of its proximity to the mythic Scots-Irish ballad tradition. Scots ballads were sung in the hills, and Parton sang those ballads, but they were not the only music being made. There was an audacity to Parton, who knew that the audience constantly mixed other traditions—they sang what they heard from their parents or grandparents, what they heard in church, on the radio, as part of printed parlor songs, field songs from sharecroppers or enslaved people, and from travelers. Audiences expected a certain kind of realness. Dolly delivered on that realness, and then, via the creation of a set of selves, extended and deepened it. She smoothed this multi-sourced melange into a singular Appalachian genre.

Understanding the failures of Dolly in the 1980s is to understand the breakdown of her high-risk/high-reward strategy of connecting ideas of authenticity to the landscape. The failure begs the question of what Dolly was straying from and thus requires an understanding of the land itself.

For country music, the past has always been disappearing, the act of recording has always been an act of making real, and making real is a commercial act. Performing realness in urban or cosmopolitan cities and transmogrifying it into pop never erases the initiating tension.

In private conversations with Charles Hughes, the adroit critic of the South, country musics, and listeners' culture, about Dolly and the authenticity, I asked a question about whether she was performing falseness as real, he reminded me of the television show *Hee Haw*. A show which policed what could be considered country but also made fun of an insider audience, insider in that they knew the small-town jokes which were slung, but insider also which told stories and sung songs about being poor but proud—there was class anxiety in *Hee Haw*.

*Hee Haw* started as a rural reworking of *Rowan and Martin's Laugh-In*, mixing vaudeville-style jokes with ongoing short sketches and musical performances. The musical performances were always first-rate, and like the radio broadcasts of the Grand Ole Opry or the Louisiana Hayride, a pretty clear measure of fame or canonicity in country music; playing *Hee Haw* meant that you were a legitimate country music star.

The stories and jokes lacked the risque double entendre of Rowan and Martin. In 1978, Horace Walker mentioned that the humor was not only rural but also defined by Appalachia. The show relied not on a general understanding of rurality as a trope but on a very specific geographic region, arguing that it (and *Petticoat Junction, Green Acres*, and the *Beverly*

*Hillbillies*) were about the Ozarks in particular, and that this depiction of the Ozarks narrowed how we understand working-class cultures. For Walker, *Hee Haw* took all of the adult pleasures out of the region and depicted them as childlike, if not stupid:

> Even *Hee Haw* continues the repeated corn of simple virtues and childish simplicity. The warmth of the fireside, the good neighborliness of the group are all combined with the cornpatch, the front porch whisky still, and the barbershop as symbols of childishness. The real vicious view is not that hillbillies and Southerners are made fun of. It is that mount and Southerners are not considered part of the adult population of the country cult. (160)

Youngness does not have to be dumb; Dolly knew from a very young age that men would think that she could be taken advantage of, because of where she was from and how she presented. In 1967, a few years before *Hee Haw*, when she was still working with Wagoner, she inverted the idea of the simple virtues. When she sings "Dumb Blonde", with its chorus of "Just because I'm blonde don't think I'm dumb/ Cause this dumb blond ain't nobody's fool," marks an explicit cleverness, if still a plain one. That the audience might think that she was stupid, but Dolly knew that she was clever.

The Ozark folklore collector Vance Randolph and the Hungarian Jewish Gershon Legman spent decades documenting the lived language of the working class. Both noted dozens of examples of city folks underestimating country folks. Randolph and Legman worked together once on a two-volume collection of Appalachian folk songs and stories, *Unprintable Ozark Folksongs and Folklore*. Some of the songs and jokes ended up in *Hee Haw* or the routines of country comedians; the form and tone of the stories were often the same, but the details had been sanitized, any filth or complex morality excised. (Leghorn was known for his two-volume study on the anatomy of the dirty joke and a three-volume collection of obscene limericks; it should also be known that in 1976, Randolph put together a collection of folk songs called *Pissing in the Snow*.).

I am not saying that *Hee Haw* is less authentic than Randolph and Legman, but rather that culture moves and flows and that all kinds of stories of hillbillies or rednecks were fed into the American culture machine. There is never one culture, and the culture pushes back insistently. There is a mutually reinforcing network of reading with the grain and against it, especially when it comes to the Ozarks and the Appalachia, mirroring actual physical places that have been mined for cultural materials like they were mined for physical materials. Parton's use of Appalachian tropes as a way of liberating herself from people like Porter Wagoner is key here—especially how much she was in on the joke or not even the joke but the story. When she sings, "this dumb blonde is nobody's fool," she makes a statement about building self—this dumb blonde, this dumb hillbilly, this dumb girl singer is smarter than you, and is more independent than the misogynist culture of Nashville would allow. How she used her landscape and herself to sell a product so ingrained in America is almost cynical.

Even though Dolly only appeared on *Hee Haw* a few times, she did this work of recontextualizing the insider/outsider performative repeatedly—in fact, her ability to extend what Appalachia could mean, in a deeply populist context, in making the dirty jokes and tragic stories of her youth into something common, of universalizing the local, was central to her success—and that she did so with such a range and depth of materials (songs, books, movies, TV movies, TV shows, streaming shows, theme parks, stage shows, talk show appearances, concerts—a mine whose ore never depletes) is almost miraculous.

This was a central narrative of Capp—the idea that Appalachian virility stemmed from their isolationism, that separation from government intervention was the cause of their idealized bodies, and that they would be at risk of being stolen by people (there are layers of irony here—Capp not being working class himself, copying working-class aesthetics, as an act of mockery, white working-class people who built their lives on stolen Cherokee land) who did not understand them. People of Appalachia, who were in reality quite connected to the rest of the world—who mined coal for tycoons, who worked on railroads whose trains ran to the coasts, who had radios, and who had newspapers—were told repeatedly of their supposed isolation.

When Parton identified with Daisy Mae on *White Limozeen*, she extended this tension of the exterior writer arguing for an Appalachian interiority.

In an infamous 1977 interview, Barbara Walters asked Parton if she considered herself a hillbilly. She responded, "We're the ones you would consider the Li'l Abner people—Daisy Mae, and that sort of thing—they took that from people like us. But we're a very proud people. People with class—it was country class, but it was a great deal of class." Walters was startlingly rude, but Parton faced the interview with grace and aplomb, explaining class and gender lines with gentle patience to someone who did not make much effort to understand (this being one example of many).

By invoking Lil Abner, Parton is saying to Walters and Holden that she understands how she is being read and, with a certain amount of needling, that the urbane people who claim to be tolerant or understand difference still have an outsider's idea of working-class people, defined by a stereotypical media property. There is a certain hint of Parton calling Waters out for misunderstanding exactly who she is.

Dolly is writing *White Limozeen* about going back to the country, back to the old region, and slipping into old patterns. She talks about moving away and calls herself Daisy Mae. There, in the title track, she allows that the hillbilly persona is at least a little bit of an act. She knows the social ease that occurs when there is no daylight between person and persona, and that there is tension in showing off Los Angeles to her people—that marking herself as Daisy Mae as a performative strategy—not simply urbane nor Appalachian, but performing Hollywood for the Appalachian crowd, and Appalachia for the Hollywood crowd—refusing the contempt of Capp for something more complex. Dolly worked in the same way that *Hee Haw* worked. She saw Hollywood's contempt for her birthplace, and she played it up. She could pretend to be dumb or Southern or both, and the money would keep rolling in.

# 2
## *White* (Emphasis on White) *Limozeen*

What goes unsaid among many critics writing on Dolly, and by Dolly herself, is the absence of race in her songs. Dolly writes as a white performer, often for a white audience, perpetuating the myth of a white Appalachia within a largely white genre. It is convenient for Dolly to pass into mainstream country success by forgetting the social context and history of race in her construction of the region—just as the imagination of people writing the myths of Appalachia, like Capp, was convinced that the hollers were always white spaces. The historian Guy Lancaster notes that there were whole runs of Black newspapers in Arkansas that were not saved or reproduced.

Reading the introduction to *Pissing in the Snow*, Vance Randolph's collection of Ozark folk tales, he mentions how important the stories were for (frankly, mostly English, Scottish, and Irish-derived) cultural communities to understand or extend social memory, and though he does not say so directly, by mentioning Black scholars who are doing similar works in eastern urban centers, he makes a shadow argument—that there were no Black people in the Ozarks or Appalachias and that folklore collection for Black people should be done by Black scholars. He thus did not spend as much time with Black subjects as he did with white subjects, and he spent almost no time with Indigenous or Latinx subjects.

Dolly spends much of her time considering the history of her people—and talks about them as existing from the beginning of Appalachia—but she does not consider the many non-white cultures that made music in the region. Speaking of her family from the nineteenth century onward, she ignores that her family fought in the Civil War. Southern white heritage rested on the violent erasure of Black people through the slave trade (though Dolly's family, fought for the union, and also was most likely too poor to own slaves), the history of segregation, and the deliberate geographical separation of white and Black people in the region.

It was not only Black people though. The scholar Susan Emeley Keefe, in her essay "Appalachia and Its People," estimates 60,000 Cherokee lived in what is now considered Appalachia before white people came to the hills of Tennessee. In the accounts of the earliest settlers, they describe being scared of these first peoples, while making a consistent effort to push them from their traditional territories.

The traditional definition of Appalachian music is a consequence of these erasures. The myth that Appalachian music is derived solely from the Scots-Irish tradition or the idea that the language of white Appalachia is closest to Irish—a history propped up by such glorifications as the region's obsession with *Ivanhoe*, Sir Walter Scott's novel of medieval Scotland which depicted the separation of Christian and Jews—has been perpetuated for centuries. It also deliberately erases the actual origins of the culture of the place—so much of it West African—from the banjo to the call and response found in Pentecostal hymnody. Dolly felt comfortable mixing genres, and her albums moved through a wide range of feelings. She even moved through Christian denominations before becoming not very Christian after all. However, with rare exceptions (Smokey Robinson's appearance on *Rainbow)*, she prioritized not only white forms, continued the whitewashing of both the Appalachian region and the music that came from there, but also other genres—her move through genres could be read as an act of colonialism.

Dolly's avoidance of race, or failing to talk about race except in the most anodyne circumstances, complicates her legacy. There are a few stories about Parton and race that make her acceptable to white liberals. In the middle of the uprisings around the murder of George Floyd, a story went around saying that the profits she made from Whitney Houston's cover of "I Will Always Love You" were reinvested in a historical Black community. The full context is a little more complex. The quote came from an appearance on the talk show, *Watch What Happens Live* with Andy Cohen. Cohen tossed her a softball question, asking her what the best thing she did with the money that she got from those royalties. Best here, I think, in the understanding of Parton, might mean most ethical, but it also means most money on return—for Dolly, the capitalist, the two are inescapably linked. She replies: "I bought a property in what was the

Black area of town and it was mostly just Black families and people that lived around there and it was just off the beaten path from 16th Avenue."

She is acting as a gentrifying landlord. 16th Ave is Music Row and is not off the beaten path from anywhere, and so she makes money off Black labor (really, twice—from Houston's cover and from the land that she purchased with Houston's money). This was not the only time that Parton could be thought to be appropriating Black labor. In an interview for *New York Magazine*, the Chic founder and disco pioneer, Nile Rodgers, critiqued her forays into disco in the mid-1980s, saying: "I would go to a club, and Dolly Parton was singing disco; it was disgusting. I hated it."[1] Rogers does not note which club or if Parton was singing in person, but the idea that Parton was borrowing what was not hers is strong here. It should be noted that there was genre policing on the other side—Loretta Lynn called Parton's work in the late 1970s "puzzling," and there were critics who called *Rainbow* "an ugly disco glop." I am not sure that *Rainbow* was disco, but it was both ugly and gloopy.

Parton tends to change her mind on race when it is financially advantageous. For decades, at Dollywood, there was a dinner show called Dixie Stampede where the Confederate and Union soldiers would theatrically battle each other until the audience decided who won. It has been reported that they often chose the Confederacy. When the details of the show became public, there was enough outrage

---

[1] https://digitalcommons.georgiasouthern.edu/cgi/viewcontent.cgi?article=2645&context=etd

that its name was changed to the Dolly Stampede. Dolly as Dixie has a certain cultural resonance.

These are contemporary examples, but Dolly has a long history of opportunism when it comes to race. In her 2017 thesis, *The Parton Paradox: A History of Race and Gender in the Career of Dolly Parton*, the adroit academic and critic Lindsey Hammer details how Parton refused to boycott apartheid South Africa at the height of political pressure for artists to avoid the morally indefensible regime there in 1982. When asked about it, she responded, "I'm an entertainer, not a politician . . . I can't speak to the problems of another country. I'm just looking forward to the tour, and I'm going to stay out of trouble." This was after significant pushback against the regime, from local communities in South Africa all the way to the United Nations.

Hammer also notes the central problem of Dolly's racial avoidance (and also her political slickness):

> The silence surrounding her participation in this event could be because she recognized it as a bad decision and was embarrassed by it; or, it could be that she does not deem it as important in the first place. Her few statements on her performance at Sun City suggests, however, that she was aware of problems within South Africa, but perhaps she was not informed as to the extent of the country's apartheid system.

Dolly is not stupid. She knows what sells, what her audience cares about, what they might not, and where the social environment shifts enough to cause her some financial scandal. She moved into disco because she thought it might make her money; she went to South Africa because she thought it might make her money; and just perhaps she pulled back on some of *White Limozeen's* genre fuckery because it was losing her money—just like Dixie Stampede.

Understanding the failure of Dolly in the 1980s is to understand the breakdown of her high-risk/high-reward strategy of connecting identities with ideas of authenticity and landscape. Dolly continues to beg the question: When she strays, what is she straying from? This requires an understanding of the landscape itself.

The complications of this intermingling of history, while at the same time being an ersatz segregationist, are explained in great depth by Charles Hughes in his book *Country Soul,* particularly in how he quotes KH Miller's *Segregating Sound.* Hughes writes extensively on Parton's ability to absorb genres outside of country to make them country—especially disco, when, for some of the 1970s, Parton became a singer of flashy, pleasurable, urbane forms. I would argue that the ability to synthesize this work exists because the cultural memory placed Parton in Appalachia and knew that she would always return. She brought Appalachia to London or Studio 54 or Los Angeles. Appalachia is coding as white here, but also working class.

Hughes directly quotes Karl Hagstrom Miller's *Segregating Sound* in that coding in the early part of the twentieth century:

This process, too, evinced the complex meaning of various southern-identified genres in the early period. Generally speaking, pop and jazz were recorded in studio settings that—in both practice and connotation—reflected their connection to urban modernity. Meanwhile, supposedly "traditional" genres like blues and hillbilly were primarily recorded "in the field" by record producers or folklorists who consciously hoped to capture the "real" sounds of the disappearing American past. (204)

Dolly has a similar anxiety about the authenticity that once grounded country music, choosing to record in the city but never forgetting the intervention of these folklorists. It might be a false dichotomy, in the early twentieth century, the splitting of genre across racial lines—the difference between hillbilly records and race records, for example, but also not an accurate representation of people's listening—think of the folklorist Alan Lomax, who refused to record songs from Tin Pan Alley or the radio. If *White Limozeen* can be seen as a corrective to the excesses of *Rainbow*, and if the thinking is that *Rainbow* was too pop, there is the uncomfortable note that too pop might mean too Black, that it betrayed the whitewashing that Dolly has done throughout her life. For example, including a duet with Smokey Robinson and the inclusion of explicit Black aesthetics, even in the late 1980s, might have been a bridge too far for the Nashville crowd. The Black critic, Tressie McMillon Cottom, in her long essay about Parton, "The Dolly Moment," notes in 2021 that Dolly has gotten away from the criticisms of the left—including but not limited to those of labor and those of queerness. McMillon Cottom says that this is especially true of race:

How Dolly has gotten away with performing so many challenged identities while completely escaping critique resonates with audiences that consume the South precisely for the hope that whiteness still matters. As for the rest of us, well, we are here for the blonde ambitions.

It is useful to note that *White Limozeen* was part of that rescue operation. She was very successful for a very long time, and then she was not as successful, and there must have been some amount of anxiety in sliding away from success.

She is performing challenging operations throughout the album—she is noting that the misogyny and classism of her previous incarnations have not disappeared. However, Parton might not have done the hard work on race, and when she gets close, she retreats from the discourses. The reviews of *Rainbow* were disastrous, and it's a bad album, perhaps Dolly's most significant failure, but the subtext of some of the reviews is telling. They were usefully collected by Stephen Miller in his 2009 biography of Dolly, *Smart Blonde*. He quotes the USA Today critic as saying, "Imagine Porter Wagoner singing 'Whole Lotta Love.'" Another unnamed critic said, "Dolly Parton doing soul makes about as much sense as Pavarotti doing country," and according to the New Musical Express, the album featured material which "should have been left in the Tina Turner songwriter's demo reject pile." (288)

Miller comes very close to making the subtext here, though he does not state it explicitly—there are two things occurring in the reaction to *Rainbow*: the first is that Dolly is far from her station and needs to be brought back into Nashville, a Nashville where men choose the material (Porter Wagoner here is not an accident), one of unadulterated genres (but the genre is always adulterated), and a move back from whiteness and class (ignoring the country's consistent, complicated, and problematic history of race). Tina Turner is especially interesting, as Francesa Royster notes in her 2022 book *Black Country*, she played country, and her 1980s success shared similar qualities with Dolly's, in terms of their shared southernness, childhood poverty, and crafting of their misery into a high camp, diva aesthetic. The difference between them can be seen in some of the domestic crises of Turner, and how they are depicted by the press. Turner's abjectness, the narrative of a comeback after being beaten by Ike, and some of the racial politics of that enter into territory which Dolly just does not go. The stability of Parton's marriage is unusual, as is how quiet Dolly is about her husband. Turner escaped from her hometown too—spending most of her last years far away from the American South—both geographically, living in Switzerland, and musically, never again trying sounds like the country albums she made in the early 1970s. Whiteness in America gives access and freedom, allows for aesthetic experiments, for an appropriating hunger that is given to no one else.

*White Limozeen* re-established Dolly as a country star, and that re-establishment was connected to a return home. She went into the world, succeeded, failed, succeeded a little more, and that success was connected explicitly to a renewed understanding of what her audience wanted. *White Limozeen* was where Dolly turned from a country artist, and a singular one, to *the* country artist, from one ambassador among a number of the rural South to the most significant one. How her voice shifted, how she used her body, how she centered one kind of experience, and how she learned to monumentalize her experiences all begin with *White Limozeen*. It's another kind of selling out after she did all that selling over.

# 3
# Regional Tensions

If *White Limozeen* is an album where she considered what her past is and made a set of historical arguments, then some of those are about her continued relationship with Appalachia, about what it means to be a Daisy Mae in or outside of Hollywood. Some of those are general genre problems, some of these are explicitly within the text, and some are ambivalent about landscape as a trope, not a specific geography. There are bits where she moves far from Appalachia, in the Texan references in "Yellow Roses," or when she talks about a romantic rival "dressing like a cowgirl's dream," in "Why'd You Come in Here Lookin' Like That"—that one line hinting that it is not only an erotic rivalry but a geographic one, impugning her authenticity, suggesting that the cowgirl look makes her less real and thus less of a legitimate object of affection.

These were just minor entries, small anxieties. The title track is the space where Parton calls herself Daisy Mae, where she presents herself not as an Appalachian figure who flirts with the genre in ways that only insiders can do, but as is now fully artificial, suggesting that succeeding in Hollywood is to capitulate to their understanding of her hometown. There is some slippage here—she talks about how she has not changed, that she is still the hometown girl. In this passage, I am reminded of the differences between Crystal Gayle and Loretta Lynn—the person born in town and the person born in the holler; here, Daisy Mae is not in the holler. She does not come from Appalachian poverty. She is from the very first step, and they're already on their home turf.

Though the song claims to be comfortable with her Daisy Mae personae, the tension between urban and rural, maybe not being comfortable in either space, means that the anxious can be seen in a strange coda at the end— her singing, then speaking, the words "white limozeen," emphasis on the z, on the drawl, and the sputter, over a long bluegrass line (the city riding over the country). Maybe she doesn't believe that she is riding here, maybe there is a bit of a punchline, or an emphasis or an abstraction, but the sheen of a well-made machine is throughout that small coda, more agile than the limousine in question. Parton always plays with the parenthetical, or the side note, eliding the meaning of the song with a wink—in the repetition of that word in the coda, there's an echo of "look at how I got out of that small town," and at the same time, an element of succeeding and refusing to apologize for that success. An inside joke with her band, and perhaps with the country music audience, who knows when she is being made fun of.

Dolly sang the title track on *Saturday Night Live* in April of 1989, giving one of the best performances of her career.

She is dressed in a skin-tight gold lame suit, shredding an electric guitar while fronting a five-piece band. Even from the beginning, she's greasier and faster than the record, committing to the bit in ways that she didn't in the studio. She struts and cats, though not through the entire stage, the first chorus comes, the band becomes louder, and she plays the guitar with a little more aggression. The title of the song is repeated by her band, one woman, two men, one Black, two white. There is an excellent performance by the pedal steel player, the backbone of the whole enterprise. The third chorus starts, with even faster-syncopated finger snaps added to the percussion.

She makes the abstract coda on the studio song an actual chorus—saying "white limozeen" five or six times before the real breakdown begins. There is a spoken outro, where she tells the audience, "I think it's only fair folks that this was not your ordinary limousine; this is one of these big stretch jobs" as Dolly fully extends her arms. Then she performs a stretch job of her own. She describes what's in that car—"a tv, a bar, a VCR, a telephone"; she talks about the "driver in the red bow tie driving through the fast food restaurants," what she would pick up at those restaurants—a full bucket of fried chicken. She licks her fingers, then describes the chicken in detail, about how greasy it is, about how she would "eat that chicken in the back and throw the bones through the sunroof." She compares the limousine to a boy back in the smoky mountains who was convinced that she would never make it and how he was driving an old, rusty pickup truck. The original broadcast stops there—but on the tape, at the Country Music Hall of Fame

Archives[1] she adds a chunk of adjectives about exactly how greasy the chicken was and how pleasurable eating it was—somewhere between the anecdote about chucking the bones out the sunroof and the mention of the bad boyfriend, she says exactly what a White Limozeen is—it's a miraculous transporting location, where the grease of the fried chicken, the grease of class, and what happens when you call blues greasy occur on this stage in New York—far from both Sevier County and Los Angeles. In this live moment, not repeated in concert or on the album, it seems out of control, but is also deeply and profoundly a good time—an in-control, blisteringly smart, this-proves-she-can-do-anything good time.

She has to be more careful on the studio version of the song, the wildness might affect how it sells. The album, then, is less anxious than the *Satruday Night Live* version. The album has to sound tight and clean, country enough without isolating the pop audience, and within the parameters of tight deadlines. The success of the album depends on her being a little polite. If the coda on the title track allows for some kind of blowout, some kind of release valve, the vulgarity of the *SNL* performance suggests a lost opportunity. Parton's skill is self-awareness, a literal move from Saturday night to Sunday morning, not entirely contained by sainthood. It feels like one of the last times she became that vulgar.

---

[1] I suspect that the Internet Archive one was cut for time. https://archive.org /details/saturday-night-live-s-14-e-17-dolly-parton.

Dolly's *White Limozeen*, which generalizes ideas of the South, plays Southern, because of her already extant skills in the North, and could sell the record as a redemption arc for leaving ideas of the South behind. On the *SNL*, where she plays the most vulgar version of the title track—there is another skit where a dozen cast members ask Dolly to tell her stories. As she begins to tell them, they tell her the punchline, sometimes snidely and sometimes friendly. On bare risers, in the middle of an empty New York sound stage, with Parton in costume and the rest in casual clothing, she admitted publicly that she has been playing Southern for a long time, and her audience knew it as well. The playing takes two forms. The first is the idea that Dolly seems to be teaching these New York actors what it means to be in the South—the energy of the skit is of students at a drama workshop listening to an instructor, whose stories have all been told. It is not the storytelling of the front porch which is usually prevalent in these depictions. The second is that it is a rehearsal space, and an unusually casual one. The cast—including David Spade and Dana Carvey, a cast that is slightly younger than *SNL* usual cast—are portrayed as upstarts slickly dismissive of an elder's wisdom—a kind of slacker aesthetic. But Parton knows that they are dismissive, and there is an odd mutually reinforcing puncturing—the cast knows it's a joke, Dolly knows it's a joke, and the joke is one of the more cynical that Dolly has ever done—one where the punchline rests on seeing the mechanics of a joke. There is a difference between everyone being in on the joke, playing along, and getting some mutual pleasure from it, and having everyone realize the jokes or stories have been told so long that they are threadbare, and unable to be repaired. The greasy live performance is one way out of it, and the theme park might be another, but on that soundstage is a barrenness that Dolly rarely allowed.

The album, how she played it in public, and how she sold it on television were the strongest evidence of her homecoming.

# 4
# Money

Dolly keeps telling us that it costs a lot of money to look as cheap as she looks, but she doesn't look cheap, and she has money. Post *White Limozeen* playing cheap but making a lot of money was the central irreconcilable break between public perception and private reality in Dolly's life.

The market here is an interesting problem, one could say that the market is about what is for sale and how it is sold. Dolly here is selling herself, and being sold, part of the Appalachian persona is poverty—as she grows older, the poverty becomes more of a joke and less harrowing. But she also talks about cheapness and its corollary, in not so many words, how much it costs to look this cheap or how she is still cheap. One of the more revealing moments is when she talks about her clothes and her wigs. In several interviews, she mentions that she has hundreds of cheap wigs (365 according to an interview with Ralph Emery Schmidt, 220) or that even if she wears the expensive ones for television or film, they end up looking cheap anyways or that she does have pricey clothes but not expensive-looking clothes. In another interview with Margaret Monynihan, she mentions that

> she spends a lot of money on cheap clothes. I don't go buy just one or two things. I can thank the Lord I can do whatever I want. I wear the same things over and over and over. I look a certain way and I like it because I'm comfortable with it. (In a 1984 interview for *Interview*)

The clothes she buys, though, are new, and they don't come from Wal-Mart.

The repeating of clothes can be seen in the repeating of stories and one-liners.

Dolly is known for being a wit, but to earn that reputation, she repeats the same bon mots over and over again—and has done so for decades. It was known this was how Dolly operated as early as the late 1970s, when Dave Hirshey, a journalist from the New York Daily News, wrote that "occasionally she'll slip and give you something different, but like Rodney Dangerfield, she has a hundred rehearsed bits, she even has a rehearsed giggle. Everything is recycled. But she didn't give me the same quotes as she did the New York Times, she knows the market."[1]

Here, she is doing two things—she is proving to the audience that she is no longer poor and that she has made it. But she is also saying that she knows how she had made it— that she was rewarded for presenting bad taste, and no one wants Dolly in good taste. Bad taste worthy of the stage costs

[1] Quoted in the Randy Schmidt edited collection of interviews *Dolly on Dolly*.

significant money, but it is money where every rhinestone and every spangle is shown. The public presentation still cares about money, money is significant, and it doesn't hide behind an old money minimalism. Warhol moves between the obviousness of new money and the genteel taste of old money, so when he plays with Dolly's image, he makes this split obvious. When he asks the descendant of a nineteenth-century family who has made it to help interview Dolly, she must know too. The chat is secretly about hidden capital (or not so secret, the first page shows exactly how much Dolly was making when she was twenty-one).

*Interview* was Warhol's house journal, and the 1984 interview was with Warhol and Maura Moynihan—the daughter of Daniel Patrick Moynihan, a Democrat, and someone who was in charge of crafting surveys about urban poverty, through a series of reports in the late 1970s and 1980s. Parton was in Warhol's circle at the time—in her mid-1990s autobiography, she talks about how her manager Sandy Gallin commissioned a 1980s portrait of Dolly. Warhol charged tens of thousands for these paintings, and they were not the most flattering—she hated them, and Gallin hated them, and, in her telling, Parton eventually either refused the commission or had Gallin refuse them. She uses the word finagled. I saw these paintings at an Art Gallery of Ontario exhibition a few years ago, they were angelic and ghostly and kitsch and not flattering, and very flattering—I can imagine if you expected the commission to be received positively, that these would startle. I wonder, in that moment, if Dolly thought she was being made fun of, that her moving between personae or personhood was being mocked—or maybe that the persona could not be fixed, that to be significant it had to physically move, and that the blankness of the portrait betrayed the movement of the body. Or I wonder if she noticed the difference between a kitsch to love and a kitsch that was being made fun of—that for once, she was not in on the joke.

Class is part of this. Warhol grew up very poor and very working class in Pennsylvania, in neighborhoods that had fairly direct connections to coal. His entire life was spent escaping those roots, not playing with them like Dolly did, but pretending they did not exist at all. There were exceptions—his relationship with his mother, his Catholicism, The Warhol portraits made Dolly's complex, performative poverty into his narrative, they erased her.

At the AGO, in front of these commissions were Warhol's wigs—it made me a little sad that in the *Interview* interview, they didn't discuss each other's wigs. Warhol grew up poor too, grew up anxious about his body, and created a persona so fake, while pretending it was real, that the anxiety was resolved in the acting that the persona was real, or at least more real than the person who was inhabiting it.

The other thing that she had in common with Warhol was this endless shopping—what Dolly refers to as endless outfits, and Warhol's infamous house filled with tchotchkes, paintings, furniture, and jewelry. For Warhol, the work he and his associates bought was either very expensive or very cheap, and the clutter which did not distinguish between either was key to his taste, perhaps the creation of a new taste. (When Warhol died, he had enough stuff gathered, it took Sotheby's three days and three over-stuffed catalogs to sell it all.) For Dolly, there was a shared moment of accretion, but Dolly refused to acknowledge that she had anything very expensive in her collection. Celebrity means that there is a kind of fairy dust that is sprinkled over everything—that things are more valuable because she is associated with them, and yet, the central anxiety of her life is one of Appalachian poverty.

This transformation from systematizing poverty to incredible wealth, but a wealth that she spreads widely, mostly to children, is central to the myth of Dolly, and there was some concern in the late 1980s that the money, and thus the resulting magic, would go away. Parton would not talk about this in public, but *Rainbow* must have lost a fortune and definitely lost her recording contract with Columbia.

This move between persona-building and personhood, selling one on the back of the other with no real assumption that either was particularly stable, is central to how she sold records. In his chapter on Dolly, in *The Persistence of Sentiment: Display and Feeling in Popular Music of the 1970s,* the Los Angeles musicologist mitchell morris does a very clever discussion of Dolly, mentioning the history of mountain music, American culture, and the life of Dolly as well—that she manages to make personal and local what had been a centuries-long, national joke, but he also notes that though there was money to be made in Nashville, it might not have been enough. No one lasts as long in Nashville, does as much as Parton does, without a shit ton of talent. We assume this with Bowie, for example, the art of working persona to please an audience, but audiences, convinced of Nashville's cult of authenticity, reward her for being real. Part of her realness is how she shifts, absorbs, extends, and plays with an audience across form and genre.

mitchell notes, in this discussion of what exactly it means for Dolly to sell out, calls the chapter "Crossing Over with Dolly Parton," and he quotes an interview she gave to *Country Weekly* in 1997:

> Before I crossed over, when I was being so totally true to country music, I wasn't making a dime. I couldn't even buy panty hose hardly . . . . People thought I was just rolling in dough because I was having these chart records. Number One records, "Coat of Many Colors", "I Will Always Love You", and "Jolene". You know what? "I Will Always Love You" sold 100 000 copies, and "Jolene" sold 60, 000 copies. "Coat of Many Colors" didn't even sell that . . . So I thought, I'm going to broaden my appeal. I'm going to have to cross over—try to get into bigger television, stuff like that. I made that choice . . . and I got crucified…at the time. People thought I'd made a major mistake. But if I hadn't done that, I wouldn't have any money now." (182)

This quote is so rich—first of all, I love crossing over, in some kind of blasphemous moment, like crossing over from this world to the next, from the Mississippi to the Jordan. I also love that she hints that there is not one country music and that being loyal to country music is a fool's errand. The thing she is worried about buying is pantyhose, instead of food or paying the rent. Then she slides into data, into actual numbers. It's almost like the folksy crossing-over talk is sugar for the pill of actual selling. She then describes selling out as an act of hospitality—that she is going to be crucified for. (I will leave the idea of Dolly as Jesus as an act to the reader.)

Dolly recognizes that being self-aware about her persona, about how she sells herself—and also notes that there is an anxiety about capital; that she made her money on learning how to present the excesses of herself as pure, or the pricey acts of acquisition as humble—of even the unrelenting ego of building a theme park to your own suffering, as an act of modesty; and people would believe you.

There is no better example of this than the title track of *White Limozeen,* not only the previously discussed idea of Daisy Mae in Hollywood or the ostentatious good taste for Nashville/bad taste for New York titular vehicle, but the idea that she is the one to guide her relations through Hollywood, the ego of self-positioning as Virgil, and even the ambivalence she feels about that city, and it's refusal to acknowledge that her life was well cushioned with money, that the depictions of the dark cities might not be what she was actually experiencing. The idea should be noted that an album of soft landings in a city which is often viewed as a contemporary Babylon might not be a successful rescue project.

But the idea of how she presents herself, that she is pretty ruthless about how she sells herself and how she calculates who she is and how to sell it is key here. It's not that the work isn't significant, she knows the songs are good, she doesn't have to engage in the false modesty of talking about the songs, she basically says, I wrote three of the best songs ever written, and I got paid jack shit, and so I moved to where the actual money was.

The movement is where things get interesting—she did this through a continued revision of self-fashioning, not just one self-fashioning, but vamping and revising and improvising from a central form—listening to a good bluegrass band playing live, where they react to each other, slowing down or speeding up depending on how the song plays, getting really soft or really loud, and improvising against the central core of a song. The best example of this, I know, is Flatt and Scruggs's "Foggy Mountain Breakdown." How every cover of that song sounds different depends on who's performing it—a little more chicken fried up North, more intimate when it is played indoors, how the live versions in the Opry sound different (less raucous, the Opry's historic prohibition of drums means that the work played there never really rocks) or that the song never quite escaped from the orchestration of Charles Strouse, using it for Bonny and Clyde in 1967. Listen to how Parton sang "I Will Always Love You" at public funerals (at Wynette's, Wagner's, and Judd's, and we damn well know she will sing it at Willie's), and see how she shifts meaning—even in that specific time and place. Parton knows what her audience wants.

Viewing Dolly as a saint means overemphasizing her service to this nebulous idea of the purity of country music and underemphasizing her desire to get paid. Viewing Dolly as an Appalachian ideal means that the discussion is about her being unchanging, a pure vessel for the spirit of country music. Part of Parton's Jebface is knowing that playing the rube or the saint for the decades before 1989 means that you can build a theme park around being part of the joke.

The gap between what Dolly says she says and what she actually has said is deeply sophisticated; there is an irony that is central to Parton. It's not only that she is part of the joke, but that she tells the joke—and that telling the joke has resulted in this empire. Everyone knows that Dolly is in on the joke, that she is playing—the dismissal of Dolly as fake is uninteresting because Dolly lets us know that both she is fake and that fakeness is a way of working toward the real.

There are, of course, other ways of dismissing Dolly, and one of them is as a camp figure—but I think that camp is an exercise for a reader who is capable of looking down on a subject and who feels just a little bit of contempt for a subject. In America, at least, there is power in the ability to craft a persona of success. If you can succeed in crafting the right narrative, that inauthentic authenticity pays out really well, not as a jackpot but in perpetuity.

Camp is what happens when the money runs out, when the project collapses, when someone is outside, and not entirely in on the joke, when the contempt cannot be hidden and cannot be weaponized; it is a mark of a subject isolated from the main avenues of taste, burrowing along the side street—it's late Elvis, or later Tammy Wynette—Dolly never had either.

The joke is key here—there is some consideration that Dolly is camp, but I think that there is a mistake in viewing camp as an act of deliberate fashioning. I think that camp is not a problem of the author but a problem of the reader—a rhetorical strategy. It occurs when the audience notes the significant gap between ambition and the delivered project. There are times when Dolly is burlesque, vulgar, or self-aware, but she knows what she is doing—the self-awareness in the shifting or changing of mode is so calculated that it lacks the failed ambition necessary to be camp. Just as *Hee Haw* is not really camp, because there is an exact correlation between what they want to deliver and what they actually deliver. The questions of camp can be answered by asking questions about who is in control, and in capitalist America, who is in control can be answered by who exactly is paying the bills.

I think that *Rainbow* could be considered camp, because its reach exceeded its grasp, that kind of wandering into the wilderness, and its failure to engage with her audience, but the bathos are absent from true camp spaces, the lack of control. I am absolutely convinced that *White Limozeen's* excesses, where they occur, are too tightly constructed to be read as anything but deliberate and pure, the burlesque of her best 1970s work, absent but absent on purpose.

If camp could be considered as then, a kind of failed ambition, and Parton's ambition rarely failed, the deliberateness of the late 1980s albums must be considered in relation to her whole career—the idea of a failed ambition exists as an answer to the question of narrative—failed from which heights, from where. That is an easy question for Dolly to answer—that *White Limozeen* can be traced in an auteurist fashion directly to 1972's *My Tennessee Mountain Home.* This ambition could be said to have a complex relationship to irony, to populism, and as it moved further and further from acknowledging poverty to acknowledging her absence (at its most base, see home versus car). *Home* has a direct relation to the land and the people in it—a song about her family doctor Robert F. Thomas, an ode to her father's boots, but also a song whose central joke is about the masochism of staying—"In the Good Old Days, When Times are Bad." What follows is the times becoming very good, the times growing larger and larger, and perhaps a kind of historical forgetting—by the time she gets around to Rainbow, with no signifiers of historical memory, the collapsing of her aesthetic could be seen as camp. The half-successful repair job of *White Limozeen* balances between the return home and the excesses of her Hollywood years—perhaps an apologia for the social climbing, definitely one that floats toward ideas of a place, again not about the place itself, not the directness of 1972.

The liminality of *White Limozeen*, the genre-agnostic, high-gloss production, pushing everything into an album which might not work, and the idea of that limozeen as one which floats across the city, which lacks the grounding of the small house that she grew up in, but also the idea that the vehicle can return her back to her roots—it's a complex, symbolic figure—and perhaps even too well thought out to be fully camp. But it is a pretty good indication of money that she is able to bring Tennessee back to LA to show herself and her success, which means any time to escape the landscape and who she is kind of fails.

# 5
# Impure Purity

If the family is one audience for Dolly's singing and the public is the larger audience, there is a middle conduit—Nashville and its industry.

The first note on the first song of *White Limozeen*, "Time for Me to Fly," is played on Paul Franklin's pedalbro (a pedal steel with a dobro resonator core assembly), and there is a solid minute and a bit of bluegrass breakdown at the back end made possible by a murderer's row of session musicians, including Vince Gill on guitar and Bela Fleck on banjo. There are a number of ways that skeptics inside of Nashville talk about artists they view as insufficiently authentic—they mention geography, Texas and Tennessee more pure than New York City, Franklin less pure than Music Row, West Texas more pure than Austin; they mention who wrote the songs or where they wrote the songs—the fewer the number of songwriters, the more pure it is; and they talk about genre—bluegrass more pure than commercial country, or instrumentation, pedal steel or banjo more pure than synths. There are also more granular distinctions, within Nashville, the most pure studio, because of its location on Music Row and because of its lineage, is RCA's Studio A. I am not sure that purity matters as much as they think it does, though.

This taxonomy of purity disregards how commercial Nashville is, how cheap and quick it is. *White Limozeen* was recorded in Treasure Island and the Lawerence Welk studios, both of which are delightfully impure spaces. By delightfully impure, I am not suggesting trashy, however we define that vexed and difficult phrase. Treasure Island studios was run by Fred Vail, a Californian who had a tangential relationship to the Beach Boys and based a career on it. The studio was in the Berry Hill neighborhood, a separate municipality about a ten-minute drive from the Ryman. It was built (depending on who you ask) in either 1980 or 1981. The studio was designed as a separation from Music Row—Vail, in an interview for the podcast *Nashville Today*, talks about how working on Music Row meant that fans would knock on the door, asking to see where Tammy Wynette and George Jones recorded. Country purity requires a kind of access to fandom, a pretending that there is no separation between fandom and artists, which Vail sought to move away from. Vail also talked about how he had an echo room, at first saying that it was an innovation, and then immediately afterwards, saying that Studio A and Studio B both had one—locations encrusted with social memory, built to resemble the classic space, to sound the same. In the decade after 1981, there were more than twenty studios near Brantford, the main road that crosses Berry Hill—so there is a community of creators above all. However, Dolly's choice to record in that space was a commercial one because it was newer or cheaper, more than anything else—a return to Nashville did not mean a refusal of commercial conveniences.

The second studio belonged to Lawerence Welk, called the Champagne Studio, after what he called his genre. Welk is part of the genre called light entertainment, hugely popular in his time, and recorded less these days, or if recorded, more ironically. The presence of studio musicians, a classic orchestra, and the choirs of Vanderbilt and Fisk meant that the dense, production-heavy music of Welk was rewarded in Nashville. He hired musicians there, and the studio that he set up eventually recorded some significant country albums by Nitty Gritty Dirt Band, Boxcar Willie, and others. Again, it is a matter of commercial convenience for Dolly and less about the purity of Nashville. The Welk Group owns Sugar Hill, where Dolly recorded *The Grass is Blue* in the 1990s, an album which was more about the purity of Nashville—this is all a complex matrix.

Given that the album was recorded under the commercial auspices of Welk, the studio musicians who played on the record were equally commercial, especially Paul Franklin.

A second-generation musician, Franklin refined his father's innovations, playing pedal steel, dobro, and the aforementioned pedalbro, among other instruments. He had in common with Parton and Skaggs an extreme precociousness, being skilled enough by the age of sixteen to perform a solo on the soft rock band Gallery's hit "Nice to be With You," which eventually sold a million copies, becoming a major hit in New Zealand, Canada, Australia, and the United States. At seventeen, he joined Barbra Mandrell's road band (Mandrell herself was a virtuoso on pedal steel), and throughout the 1970s and into the 1980s, he worked for Nashville mainstays, including Dottie West and Jerry Reed. He moved on to session work in the 1980s, working with a wide swath of artists, including but not limited to Shania Twain, Alan Jackson, Brooks and Dunn, and Rhett Atkins.

Franklin's most significant contribution is not necessarily a signature sound but the ability to shift sounds according to the needs of the audience or performer. There is something strange about his playing on *White Limozeen*, in that, an artist like Franklin, who excelled with the chameleon quality of studio production, is the most audible on the record—the first sounds that you hear are his pedalbro, and listening carefully, he peeks through in places where other instruments rest, playing through in a way typical of country arrangements, and done very well here. By comparison, the distinctive sounds of Bela Fleck's banjo or Vince Gill's vocals are more hidden. Franklin, thus, is a perfect conduit, working symbiotically between the larger public and the locked circle of the studio.

The team of musicians was assembled by Ricky Skaggs, another child prodigy turned Music Row mainstay. Skaggs spent enough time in Ralph Stanley's band before becoming legendary as a front man, meaning that bands trusted him, but he had enough authority to hire and fire. Dolly's choice of Ricky Skaggs was explicitly about returning to home, to the genre, and to the region. In an interview with the journalist Lawrence Grobel as the album was being recorded, she talks about her problems with her label, her dissatisfaction with the music she had been making, and about the geography that Skaggs and she had in common, "Rock people don't want me to do country, and country people don't want me to do rock. So whenever I would do country and rock it turned out to be 'crock!' I'm sick of it, so I'm doing pure country as part of my deal with CBS." (257)

This story has the whiff of the half-truth, a complex admission of her failures, and a spin about the possibilities of an album not yet finished. The album did not end up being a bluegrass album—a move that she would not attempt until *The Grass is Blue* in 1999. There is an idea that she returns back to her country roots when she feels like her work is not as successful as it could be. I am not sure that country was ready for a pure bluegrass album at that point—though Skaggs would be the one to give it to her. There is something moral in how Grobel talks about this return, something almost evangelical. She knew that she had moved away from her hometown, her genre, and herself, but she knows that she will have to deny all of that in order to return home, a moment of exile that she hopes to be redeemed from. It's generic though, saying, "She's aware of the mistakes she has made with previous albums." These albums must include the universally derided *Rainbow*, but wouldn't include *Trio*, from 1987, which was a more traditional country record than she had ever produced, or *Real Love*, with Kenny Rogers—not her best work, but lovely in its way (and it gave us "Islands in the Stream"), and one that sold well, or *Burlap and Satin*, from 1983, which might have been the start of this merging of country and other populist forms. Is Grobel saying that Dolly considers these albums mistakes?

She also calls it a rock album and says that no one wants it. But, her deal with CBS was for half pop albums and half country albums, and her work has always skirted between genres—she had a number of very successful hits that flirted (or completely capitulated) to disco ("Two Doors Down") or rock (her version of "Mule Driver") or gospel or any number of other genres—audiences wanted the plausible deniability that Dolly was pure country, but they were also almost always willing to go along with her—her hiring of Skaggs was then an argument in favor of this plausible deniability, but perhaps less purity than his reputation would suggest. Skaggs has become more conservative politically and musically as the years go on, but at that point in time, he was making arguments about how wide country could be.

In fact, further on in the interview, she talks about exactly what Skaggs brought to the table:

> I got Ricky Skaggs to produce the album. He had a better understanding of who I am, because he grew up in eastern Kentucky, very similar to the way we did, and his people are like my people. He knows that Appalachian music, the Irish-English-Dutch influence that came there to the Appalachian mountains. And I felt that if I was gonna do a true country album in a big way again, it was important to have somebody who has an understanding of my roots, all of them—bluegrass, country, the mountains, the gospel— not just country music as we've come to know it. (266)

In the space of three sentences, Parton is making one point and then almost capitulating on it—seeking a bluegrass album and then arguing she is also making an album where country is messier, where it is filled with a number of origins, where it does not have a distinctive sound. She is not sure if the album will be a success—you can see it in Globel when they talk about the failed variety show, and she says that "I won't feel like a failure," but he doesn't directly quote her about how she considers those albums. The inclusion of Skaggs was a return to tradition; him producing this album was an explicit refutation of the urban qualities of especially *Rainbow*.

Robert Christgau, the dean of American Rock critics, said this about *White Limozeen* in 1989:

> The crossover that marked her new label affiliation never got to the other side, so she lets Ricky Skaggs call the shots—these days he's commercial. Except on the Easter song, he cans the production numbers, and since she can still sing like a genius anytime opportunity knocks, her most country album in years is also her best. Of course, even genius country singers are dragged by ordinary country songs. And though the borrowings are better-than-average, she no longer writes like a pro without help—here provided by, such is life, Mac Davis.

There are a number of things wrong with this characterization of the album. Dolly never thought that there were two sides, her work and her voice slid through genre and class for her entire life, through medium too. She had success in film and some genuine breakthrough hits in her Los Angeles year, and though there was some slick pop work, there were also traditional songs with Emmylou Harris and Linda Ronstadt. Skaggs was commercial, and Dolly was wise to choose him, but Dolly and Skaggs worked together, just like Dolly worked together with the band. Part of it was that I think she believed in collaborative labor, that she understood how the band worked, and that it was a mutual effort toward a singular goal. You can see this in how Christgau claims that Parton sings like a genius, and she does—she has a great voice throughout this record, but that only functions because the rest of the band is so hot and tight. The genius is a collaborative one. There are also some places where this is not a country album, in the same way, that he is right that it is her most country. Genre, perhaps, can only be determined in context—in the interaction between performers, in the studio, where they agree which genre is being played, or when that agreement debuts in front of an audience who all agree that they are listening to one genre, at least in that time and place—for the length of a show, an album, or even a song. This is also why he thinks that having other writers on this track lessens her skills or abilities, denying how Nashville, at its most company town, refutes the notion of a singular author. In the studio, Dolly is first among equals, they are there because she is. Christgau suggests in his review a common trope in writing about women in country music—they depend on male songwriters, producers, or bands to fully succeed. This misogynist canard is deeply untrue.

When I listen to *White Limozeen*, I think about Skaggs's version of the song "Country Boy" from 1983. Originally performed by the English guitarist Albert Lee, who performed the guitar in Skaggs's version, it's an incredibly complex, dense, bluegrass picking pattern with only a few lyrics, mostly "I'm just a country boy at heart." For the video, Skaggs could have had anyone, he could have gone the country roads route or the nostalgic return back to his hometown, but instead, he goes to New York City. Over a period of a little more than three minutes—the people who could be country boys, even in New York City, included Albert Lee and Skaggs, but also the mayor Ed Koch, various city folks on the subway, including a Black child (there is something delightful in the Black child dancer, a moment of game noticing game) and in the middle of an instrumental section, Charlotte d'Amboise and several other dancers performed a routine which seems very Alvin Ailey-inspired. If d'Amboise, a second-generation ballet dancer, New York City native, and Tony winner for Bob Fosse's *Chicago*, could be a country boy, then anyone could be, again, against the purity of the genre. (At the very start of the video, Skaggs's Appalachian-coded elderly uncle says that the people at home are worried about him, that he was above his raising.)

What "Country Boy" and *White Limozeen* share is how they flow through the binary of country and city. Returning back to that first track, the impurity of the source material is made clear. "Time for Me to Fly" is a song by REO Speedwagon. She and Skaggs are taking the middle American rock and roll specialists and using their substantial skills, their knowledge of the genre, and an all-consuming appetite. Even on an album that is supposed to argue for a neo-traditionalism, Skaggs and Parton allow that the genre is wider than purists might think. This question of what the genre is, and what it means, is imbued not only in REO or Skaggs but also in how much Mac Davis is on this album. Skaggs provided one understanding of the country music genre, history, and context; the countrified translation of Speedwagon is another, both embodying a kind of formal overtaking of the sentimentality that was almost a disaster. Mac Davis, who had been in the business as long as Dolly provided a less self-conscious performance about the genre.

The song "Time for Me to Fly" is a kiss-off—a song about having enough of jealousy, falseness, and "intolerance." It is also a banjo rave-up, and the jubilation of Dolly's freedom from a feckless lover has a liberatory joy. When she sings "fly," she quotes, in her phrasing and her devotion to old-school forms, something like "I'll Fly Away," the gospel standard. Another joyous thing about Dolly, and about the genre, is the sanctification of thoroughly secular texts. The old gospel song is about waiting, hoping for something to come forward— the hymn begins with "some bright morning, when this life is over, I'll fly away . . . " but Dolly is arguing that she will fly away, not on some bright morning, not in some kind of cosmic eventuality, but now, and not to "God's celestial shore," but to something less ethereal. The immediacy of the track is what is vital, it's that she will fly away right now. It's also a song that almost any of her more traditional listeners would know, being around since 1929 and actively part of the sacred repertoire of the Nazarenes, Baptists, and Pentecostals. It is a place where the Baptist Skaggs and the Pentecostal Parton could meet, but it is also a song which is a strong part of the country canon—being performed by George Jones, The Stanley Brothers, and others.

Maybe a little blasphemous, but tucking this Christian reference into a very secular song is a small example of what Dolly does on this album—she sanctifies the secular and secularizes the sacred. It might also be a core understanding of Parton in general.

Thinking also about her unhappy relationship with her label and the failure of *Rainbow*, the song seems to be coded against the label. When she sings lines like:

> But I just can't get any relief
> I've swallowed my pride for you
> Lived and lied for you
> But you still make me feel like a thief

The song might be about the failure of her and a romantic partner, but also between her and the label or between her and the genre itself. Dolly widens what relational feelings can be; part of it is that her love songs and her breakup songs are always abstracted. She is quiet about her biography, and she has been in a seemingly happy marriage for more than fifty years. The songs which could be about marriage or about love, the ones that seem most biographical, Dolly has said herself, are not biographical—thinking of course, of "I Will Always Love You," which is apparently about her commercial breakup with Porter Wagoner. That she sang "I Will Always Love You" during her final appearance on Wagoner's show and that she considered it a breakup song about this commercial relationship suggests there is precedent for "Time for Me to Fly." Dolly is too much of a professional to put something out like the Sex Pistols' "EMI" or Elvis Costello's "Radio, Radio", but some of the hidden/buried anger on *White Limozeen*, appears to be transference–her most significant relationship in the last decade was one with labels and movie studios.

This relationship includes what must be a grinding talk show circuit. In 1989, between May and December, or between the end of the promotional cycle for *White Limozeen* and the beginning of the cycle for the film *Steel Magnolias*, Dolly appeared on the *Tonight Show* at least three times. Archives hide as much as they reveal. After spending ten or fifteen hours looking through press clippings, studio memos, PR guidelines, and the like from the late 1980s at the Country Music Hall of Fame, there is quite a bit of information about canceled tour slots in 1982, an ill-advised Vegas run, her health crises from 1982 to 1984, the making of *The Best Little Whorehouse in Texas*, some reviews of *Burlap and Silk*, the press pack for *Rhinestone*, and a number of documents about her opening up Dollywood.

The rare mentions of *White Limozeen* are found at the very end of official discographies provided by labels, noting that it sold well, and the first single "Yellow Roses" did alright too, but none of the conversation about the album— none of the meta-chatter that followed Parton around for years is included. There is the odd review and some wire service notices, but less than you might think. And when she appears on television to talk about the album, she is as likely to talk about the upcoming *Steel Magnolia*s, or especially the theme park.

It might be that she knew that the money would come from the theme park much longer than it came from the album, or that she thought the work was more significant one way or the other.

I looked at tapes at the Paley Center and tried to scrounge what I could on YouTube, but finding coverage from the *White Limozeen* album cycle was difficult. Not everything is on tape, not everything is digitized, when things are on tape or digitized, there are often formatting errors. That said, there is something instructive in her appearances for Carson in November of that year, which might reflect a small amount of what she is feeling in the middle of a grinding tour schedule.

The first thing to note is that the construction of a persona is a job, and for women, a pink-collar one. Especially with someone like Parton, whose entire public work consists of being likable, of ingratiating herself into the public, she is convincing her audience that she likes them, personally, on an individual level. The back and forth of the talk show, a highly artificial medium, is another act of public performance which shows less than we think it does. In fact, a talented public performer can make a viewer think they know more about the performer than they really do. We only know as much as Parton is willing to tell us, and she is willing to tell us very little. She is there to sell the opening of Dollywood, or an album, or a TV movie, or whatever else she is pushing that month. She is above all pushing the idea of Dolly. The appearances are successful when she plays at being real, while only showing what she intends to sell.

Her comfort on Carson's show was a set of performances which were outside of time and place. I mean, there was a studio in Los Angeles, and you could tell what was going on in the world by the xenophobic jokes, and the media properties that were being promoted shifted in time, and so there was some note that time had moved on. However, watching Parton on the couch and knowing that she and Carson had met four or five times a year for thirty years, they had smoothed their relationship into a kind of give and take—not quite shtick, but not far away from it. There is something purgatorial and anxious about how they circle around each other, a moment of soft parry, then a semi-ironic corrective.

Lee Solters, her press agent, was responsible for booking her on talk shows. Her press agent was an old-school agent—who worked endlessly—for 300 Broadway shows, the Beatles in 1964, Frank Sinatra for decades, Cary Grant, Carol Channing, and for Mae West. Reporters, according to his *New York Times* obit, claimed that he "gave good talk," and was known for his one lines. There is something elegant in Solters's commitment to the behind the scenes one-liner that can correspond to Dolly's warmth turned wicked or Carson's wit turned analytical.[1]

Watching her 1989 appearances, in what would be a tumultuous year for Dolly, in the middle of a machine which almost seems automatic, a few things become clear. Carson is an ironist—he is cool, and he is high-masc, not quite butch, but good at controlling the tone. We never quite know how he is feeling. Parton is earnest, warm, and empathic, and she is a high femme. Her persona is very much connected to a gender performance that rests on soothing. They both know that they are explaining their lives to people using these lenses. Part of that explanation is flirting, concealing, and subsequent revealing. In an appearance in December, Carson asks questions about Christmas, and Parton tells the same stories, about her brother being born, about being envious of her city cousins, about Tennessee. Carson offers

[1]https://www.nytimes.com/2009/05/22/theater/22solters.html

nothing in return—does not discuss the Christmases of his childhood, does not discuss the Christmases that he has now, and doesn't mention his children. He becomes an audience for her sentimentality, and because she has a record to sell, he allows her to perform it.

In an appearance supporting a disastrous TV movie with Gary Busey (the movie was shot in the late 1980s and released in 1991, it was not a success), Carson, through winks and nods, deftly makes a joke about Parton's body before noting the censors and making the joke again. There is a stark difference between Parton crafting her own body, joking about her own assets—and noting they are assets—versus Carson noting it. She sells her body, her construction of gender and self, she knows which way the games are being played, however, there is something quietly devastating about seeing her in this space, even after almost three decades, in a moment of vulnerability and, with good graces, being the subject of yet another barrage of tit jokes. Carson can only see her in a very limited way—as domestic, as a sexualized body, as a hillbilly. Carson's jokes marked the values of twentieth-century Middle America—and when conversing with Dolly, those values included classism and misogyny.

Maybe the ennui of *White Limozeen*, how the songs were often about heartbreak and leaving, was done because so much of country is about heartbreak and leaving, but maybe it's also a heartbreak about leaving or wanting to return to country from the mainstream because she was taken seriously as an artist and writer in Nashville. The Warhol paintings and the Carson appearances were just two examples of how she continued to be mocked.

It seems significant that at least five tracks on *White Limozeen*—"Yellow Roses," "Why'd You Come in Here Lookin' Like That," "Time for Me to Fly," "What Is It My Love," and "Slow Healing Heart" are directed to old lovers, a mix of sass, jealousy, personal liberation, and a little touch of anger—maybe these songs are their own way of making genre though—the heartbreak song, in all of its various iterations, is here, because it wouldn't be a country album without them. Dolly's tremulous vocals rise and fall, like the hymn singing that she did on her previous records, and she drops the final consonant in ways she always did. She knows how to raise the key, like she is back in church. As stated before, the work is filled with genius session musicians, ones who know the history of the form.

One of the people who knew that history the best was the singer Mac Davis. She had a duet with Davis on "Wait 'Til I Get You Home." Davis had been working in Nashville for decades before 1989 and had a long-standing professional history with Parton, their intimacy could be seen throughout the song.

Mac Davis grew up in Lubbock, went to high school, graduated early, and got out of town as soon as he could—first to Atlanta, at sixteen (a prodigy like both Dolly and Skaggs), where his mother lived, and later on to Nashville, there in the mid-1960s. He was signed by Nancy Sinatra's record company, Boots Entertainment (interesting to note that Sinatra was situated in Nashville and considered herself in some ways a country music singer). He wrote a string of hits, including "In the Ghetto," "Friend, Lover, Woman, Wife," "Home," and "It's Such a Lonely Time of Year."

From this point on, Dolly worked consistently with Davis from 1969 until 2019, where he had a cameo in an episode of *Heartstrings* as a preacher, Reverend Riggs. It's important that Davis and Dolly worked together, in that they were both consummate professionals, that he was part of a cluster of writers and artists that she worked with after her breakup with Wagoner. They did a week of gigs at the Painters Mill Music Fair in Maryland in 1977—the ads from the show have Dolly as the "special guest star" of Davis and Davis headlining throughout the week.

There is a moment in Davis's 1979 christmas special where Dolly is a guest and talks about being alone for Christmas for the first time. Davis concurs (they are together, alone in a cabin, obviously filmed, the emotion both genuine and a simulacra of the genuine). This small chatter moves into a recording of "White Christmas," almost cursory, excellently sung, but with less emotion than other covers. Then, the song moves to "Two Doors Down," an anthem of sexual liberation previously noted not as a country song but as a disco one. The incongruity between the tradition of "White Christmas" and the anti-tradition of "Two Doors Down" would be a mirror of what they would end up doing on *White Limozeen*.

They presented at the CMA 1980, where they listed the people who were on the show—Mac Davis going through a list of women—Anne Murray, Loretta Lynn, Crystal Gayle; Dolly claims Burt Reynolds, calling him "gorgeous, gorgeous." Then she says to Davis, "Don't worry, old flames can't hold a candle to you," and Davis responds, "Baby, I'm burning."

Dolly is, of course, intertextually quoting her current hit. They are flirting at an industry event, no one is taking it seriously, it doesn't mean anything, or if it means anything, it means the selling of a record or two—the point of the CMAs in the first place. It's interesting that they are selling Reynolds as a country star, his film work post-*Deliverance*, an attempt at redneck chic or good ol' boy apologetics, and he would soon star in *Best Little Whore House in Texas*.[2]

Davis knew Dolly was capable of moving into larger audiences for a few weeks in the late 1970s, was actually bigger than Dolly, and had been working with Dolly since the late 1960s. It makes sense that she would hire him for "White Limozeen," and the two songs that he wrote for the album tie up some of these themes. The first is the title track, which he cowrote, and the second was "Wait 'Til I Get You Home," one of the sexiest songs that Dolly ever sang—a song whose eroticism was blatant and not wrapped up in sentiment or jokes.

Maybe the Davis duo complicates the rest of Dolly's career at this time. If one of the ways of returning home, is to hire someone like Skaggs to add authenticity with his bluegrass bonafides; and another way is to make rock sound gospel, to record songs about returning home and other tracks about the ambivalence of city living, another must be to note your loyalty. Working with someone for more than twenty years, with deep devotion, means that no matter what games Dolly was playing with authenticity or how she

[2]https://www.youtube.com/watch?v=33GyphBCkXY

---

commercialized her history, she also went out of her way to have a continuance with the people she performed with. Gallin and his slick set may be a new kind of manager, but people like Davis still stuck around.

# 6
# Back to Whose Country?

If the album's title song is liminal—between the city and the country, between nostalgia and the future, the rest of the album works out problems of home, the idea of home, or of country more than specific geographic locations. There is a false dichotomy then—on one side, the city as toxic and the country as bucolic, as aesthetically and morally pleasing. There are a handful of songs on the record, where this kind of arcadia is built out of a kind of nostalgia, in the Christian heritage, a peaceable kingdom.

Nashville has always had an urban edge, it has always been about the creation of both an urban and a rural space—it's a genre that knows specifically about cities. It is also a place to do business—an isolated center of studio spaces, an isolated pod, perhaps like her time in Los Angeles. Leaving the city or going back to the city was part of a loop, one that held economic and social baggage.

Thus, *White Limozeen* is a sorting-out of the last twenty years of the genre and an explicit homecoming. The fascinating thing about this homecoming is how several kinds of nostalgia operate simultaneously: "White Limozeen" (the song) with its cosmopolitan urbanity, "Take Me Back to the Country" with its back-to-the-land Edenic bucolicity, and "The Moon, the Stars and Me" with its great cosmic sadness.

This might be a homecoming record, but it's one which starts in Los Angeles and never really leaves the mindset of Los Angeles, even when Parton is in places smaller and more local. The title track is dense with referents, dense with the possibility of bilocating, with the refusal to have a completely solid identity. The title song is an urban song—not sleazy, not that kind of urban, but one which fully recognizes the pleasures of the big city. These pleasures include the possibility of anonymity, ways to solve most physical desires, being able to reinvent or reinforce types, and showing off to guests from out of town. These are a flaneur's pleasures dependent on being able to disguise oneself. On the title track of this record, Dolly is in full-fame mode, not in disguise at all.

The song is anonymous, and the song is vulgar. The title is vulgar (in its most populist sense)—a white limousine, not a black town car—the car of arrivistes, of the nouveau riche. And not even a white limousine, a limozeen—written in country spelling, making a wink and a nod to her hillbilly roots—what she dreams of is not tasteful but explicit. The front cover of the album shows Dolly in the middle of the composition, with an audience on the right and a red carpet on the left. The composition runs on the diagonal, cut off by said *White Limozeen*, literally separating her glamorous life, from a working-class base. That Dolly is wearing a skin-tight, beaded white gown, and draped in white furs, brings the point home. (In fact, she is dressed a lot like Mae West, a figure who had no interest in the country, and a person represented by a mutual press agent, Solters).

Before she sings the title phrase, a pedal steel grinds and bucks, pushes the story forward, a little lurid, accentuating the vulgarity of the lyrics. Parton tells the story of how she got to Hollywood. Well, not how she got to Hollywood, it's important to remember that she is playing an archetype here: the starlet fresh off the bus, the blonde wanting to get into the business. The starlet is naive though, and the guitars and Dolly's pure brass vocals are self-conscious—that's the first juxtaposition of the song—the one between the naivety of the lyrics and the almost vaudeville singing style.

Parton's Daisy Mae in Hollywood is not without struggle and succeeds despite it, not because of it—the second verse mentions some of this paradox. Growing up in rural Tennessee, where the only public release may have been church songs, talk about unmitigated pleasure is rare. She invokes hard work, fighting demons in the city of angels—but there is no real change in the instrumentation—the guitars don't speed up, the vocals don't drop, and there aren't fiddles that quote Charlie Daniels. The struggle exists because the genre of the song requires one—the social spaces of Dolly's listeners, the habitus of her audience wants the success, but cannot imagine it without some kind of cosmic struggle. To desire Hollywood, but to recognize that Hollywood might be corrupt, exists throughout this mythology.

Dolly then sings of the character in the song (not Dolly, whose ambitions in Hollywood came after a successful run in Nashville and New York and who recorded this song at the tail end of a successful film career), exactly what kind of hopes he has, namely to be successful materially, not spiritually. She's singing about someone who wants to be unapologetically famous. She doesn't want to be a successful songwriter who achieves fame via the subtlety of her artistry. In the chorus, she states that "With a vision of her name in lights/ Reflecting off the cars."

She makes a moral argument in the song as well, when she sings, "Now she's living her dreams like a movie queen/ Diamond rings and all things good." There is so much going on in these two lines—a movie queen, which might mean that the person is successful in acting, like the other blondes—see Lana Turner at Schwabs,[1] or Pamela Anderson at those BC Lions' games.[2] She fully embodies this trope, even when the culture had moved on, realized the danger of the idea, or realized that it just didn't work like that at all. She also notes that her desire for material goods, which would be impossible to find in the holler, are not only delightful in a material context but also a moral good. They don't look nice or aren't fine, but the word "good" holds a heavy moral weight.

If "White Limozeen," the song, expressed a desire not to go home or even have home come back to her, then "Take Me Back to the Country" was the exact opposite. The idea

---

[1]This was obviously a myth, perpetuated by the studios, but the story is that Lana Turner was discovered in a tight sweater, sitting at the soda counter, in Schwab's Drugstore, Sunset and Crescent: https://oldlarestaurants.com/schwabs-pharmacy/

[2]https://lionbackers.com/pam.html The most complete story of Pam Anderson and the BC lions is available at this fansite.

of going back to the country and leaving the city is the exact opposite of "White Limozeen," the song—that both are on the same album is one of a number of complex juxtapositions, a refusal to settle into one ideological category. However, the songs share another similarity—they are archetypal.

The singer, who spent her previous album talking about how hungry she was for mainstream, typical success, talks now about how city life is too busy. She talks about how "there's dirt in the air and crime in the street." She is not talking about Hollywood here, but a generic city, and perhaps the whole idea of urbanity and the impossibility of nature in the big city. Here, this idea of urbanity is made even more clear, she mentions eagles, high trees, and her fishing hole. She then continues singing about how the city has too much work (what sounds like office work) "I'm sick of the clock, sick of the phone." The back, as in return to the country, is an important distinction here, there is an aching that she can return to where she was before, which turns the nuance of her lived experience into an imagined Southern paradise.

This return to the land reflects the contemporary political will and the demographic shifts of a country music—see Reagan, with his tough-on-crime rhetoric, his white picket fence bromides, the black-and-white morality of his cowboy acts; and how he played Hollywood. As Martinez reminds us, country's audience at this moment was increasingly suburban and upper middle class.

There is something (perhaps accidentally) political in Parton's reading here—being able to travel throughout Hollywood in that perfect vehicle, parading her family through those neighborhoods, and never actually leaving home—and when thinking of Hollywood outside of the idea of the *White Limozeen*, in the title track, considering it almost demonic. If I were being cynical, I would assume that Parton's years in Los Angeles were marked by studio work (film, recording, television)—rehearsals with other stars and recreation within a very specific social set. There is little evidence that Parton spent time in working-class neighborhoods in the city that she sings of here—and the passage thus lacks writerly detail.

This is especially true of her life with Sandy Gallin. Gallin and Partin co-produced more than twenty movies and TV shows, most of which were relatively successful. Gallin's circle was largely gay, though glass closeted. I cannot imagine that people like Calvin Klein, Barry Diller, Diane Von Furstenberg, or David Geffen had any interest in going back to any country outside of Malibu. (It also suggests a move away from her husband, who most likely didn't travel with her to Los Angeles, though Parton went back and forth, tricostal, if you consider the Mississippi a third coast.) Jesus, what did she and Geffen talk about? Did they trade music anecdotes? Even more excitingly, did they trade mix tapes?!

Dolly's old-school country charms, and her ease in the city, is the central tension of the album then. It refuses to settle between one or the other. This album frustrates, something that does not quite sort itself out—maybe it's the lack of specificity, maybe it's a kind of flirting with the ideological and not really committing, maybe its being a mishmash of covers and cowrites means that what Dolly intends is never quite known, and maybe it's just the general anxiety of a transitional moment. For the first time, Dolly's odes to the South lacked writerly detail, but she wasn't that specific about Los Angeles either.

Or there would be anxiety if the song was substantial in any way. "Back to the Country" races through its run time, a little over two minutes, it runs fast as well—no place to rest, even when she throws it to the band, they race through the song with lightning-quick riffs. There is an ironic gap between what the lyrics say and what the music sounds like. Here, the riffs is dense and almost frantic—it sounds exactly the opposite of the restful quality that Parton claims she wants. It's also music, which requires a number of musicians—though she does mention wanting to be alone and then mentions she wants to be with her family on this record, the family is again an abstraction.

"Back to the Country" is cowritten by a woman named Karen Staley, who grew up in Georgetown, Pennsylvania. Georgetown was small, had a population of about 208, and was dedicated to the church—a church that Staley grew up playing in. However, the town was closer to Prine than it was to Parton. Literally, the story of the coal mine and the industrial disaster was common in this part of Appalachia. The largest coal mine waste slurry deposit was next to her town. She had good luck with her career before Parton, including time in a small West Virginia Wesleyan college winning a country music songwriting contest in Wheeling. The prize was a gig writing for a contemporary Christian label in Los Angeles. She moved for the gig, but the label went belly up before she had a chance to write for them. So, the record has a double return to Los Angeles, a double mark of Southern California's failure—which might explain its Arcadian abstraction.

Maybe the track is slippery, lacks the significance of Parton's other work, because it isn't entirely Parton's song—though she sings like it might be. Nostalgia, in how it uses sentimentality, how it is an interpretive strategy, has some of the same shadings as camp, maybe even in how it cannot be determined by the author—but only comes through the reader. Nostalgia is a sweetened, falsified memory, and is often done by the hip boys, who think of themselves as Nashville outsiders, people like Prine and Jennings.

The third, back to the land, Arcadian song, "The Moon, The Stars and Me," moves between this devotion and isolation to the idea of the country in a more direct way than any other song on the album. It's a song that is so abstracted, reduced to the absolute basic facts, and it depends on the reader—the simplicity and the longing, for a man, or for the country, or the idea of both is either so simple or so generic that it depends on the listener to insert their own meanings. The song has a filigreed, silvery, small guitar—picked, not to show off, but to indicate fragility. However fragile the track is, and no matter how spare it is, it has a full band. The song gives me shivers, it's pretty in a way that is almost sublime and decorative in a way that slides into art. It has Mac McAnally's piano, Terry Crisp's steel guitar, and even some backing vocals.

She almost whispers. It's a breakup song, but one where she doesn't push up or push over. In the song, she talks about exhaustion, about not having feelings, about being abandoned, and about being hurt. For a song this simple and compact, the moments of surprise are intense. The first is how cold she is—regardless of whether Dolly is angry or frustrated, she is rarely cold. The audience contract requires a kind of warmth—even when she kisses off Los Angeles for the country, she has good things to say. In this song, she refutes any warmth:

> And what about all of those warm tender nights
> Did they mean nothing to you
> And where are the feelings I thought that we shared
> Or have you forgotten them too

What we have left is this feeling of abandonment. Dolly tells us, in a singularly pagan moment, that the lover in question has not lied in front of God, but in front of the moon, and the stars—there is an odd moment of poignancy, even in a moment that could be read as clichéd (how many songs are there about the moon, how many songs about the winter, how common is the sentiment between the coldness of a lover and the coldness of the weather—everyone from Procol Harum to Tori Amos), but Parton's authorship, via performance, sustains an old idea, not through novelty, but through a set of formal traditions that nods to the bluegrass of people like Skaggs, her own upbringing, and also to her feelings.

I cannot help but think, like other songs on *White Limozeen*, that the emotion read on the surface of Parton is a legitimate reading—she makes sure that the coldness, the fragility, the presence, is here; made more so by the favor trading, the background details, and the performances which occur here.

I believe that Dolly wanted to return to the country. I also believe that ideas of Arcadian paradise sell, and thus, a generalized Arcadian paradise sells much better. I also suspect that she loves the country when she gets there. I also suspect that she doesn't get there very often.

# 7
# What's So Traditional About Neo-traditionalism?

Authenticity in country is a constant fight about which sounds are pure, which lyrics are allowed, and which ideas are taboo. Artists are punished for not being authentic enough, but authenticity is defined by shibboleths, insider/outsider signifiers, or game playing as much as being a direct rule. A country song can be thought to be false because it has strings or because the strings are too slick; it can be thought to be impure because of the absence of pedal steel; and for a substantial chunk of the Grand Ole Opry's history, the presence of drums made it completely inauthentic. Also, sadly, for most of the genre's history—women were thought to be less authentic than men, and people of color were considered less authentic than what was assumed to be white sounds—though the banjo had West African roots, and the genre itself, from Jimmy Rodgers onwards, was marked by a melange of sounds, by a refusal of one narrative. Women were at risk of being seen as inauthentic because, via hair and costume, they were assumed to be performing their gender and thus their music more than living in it. The assumption was that men were not playing their gender at all, and even at its most decorative, the Nudie suits, for example, were butch despite and not because of their presentation. Watching Dolly's talk show appearances, there were constant jokes about her appearance and the same anecdotes about her poverty, allowing her to be taken as a joke, excused by the grinding Appalachian poverty. There were times throughout her life she was pushed against the expectations of male performers—when she first worked with Porter Wagoner, the split in the early 1980s, when she moved from Nashville to Columbia, and in the 1980s, when everything collapsed against the onslaught of the so-called neo-traditionalists.

The performance of authenticity could be considered as the only legitimate claim of the form—that to pretending to be authentic was the only legitimate way to be authentic

Dolly had some bona fides: she was born in the right place, she for a while, she told the correct jokes about her upbringing, she hired the right musicians. As discussed earlier, she even had the right gender play—she was femme enough, in the right ways to both make fun of what Nashville expected of her and to embody it perfectly. 1989 was a year where the authenticity wars crested yet again, with a movement called the neo-traditionalists moving from upstarts to mainstays. This happened at the same time that Dolly's performance of authenticity failed.

Neo-traditional artists, from the early 1980s onward, dressed, played, and had politics like they were from the 1950s, an aesthetic which could be seen in concerts, on magazine covers, in award shows, and on record. They actively looked backward, foregrounding monogamy to both women and to style. They had none of the irony of Dolly, none of the ability to move forward from one direction or another, and their music, at its best, lacked the ambivalence to form that many country musicians had in the 1970s or 1980s. If anyone could claim to sound authentic, then these artists could. Straight men perform their gender as much or more than anyone else, and though some critics include women like Patty Loveless or Reba McEntire as neo-traditionalists, I would argue that their presence was mostly a punishment of ambitious women, and sought to exclude them, often from the Neo-Trad albums, their stages, and their milieu.

It's not exactly that Dolly failed commercially, but throughout the 1980s, she had a lesser presence compared to these men. An example can be seen in the 1989 CMA Awards—the CMA tries to be all things to all subgenres of country music—and this performance had a handful of women performing, but the first performance was George Strait's western swing number "Ace in the Hole," and that mood continued through the evening. It was also hosted by Kenny Rogers and Anne Murray—these are unstable categories, and nothing is perfect; also, the Nitty Gritty Dirt Band dedicated their award to Mother Maybelle Carter.

In that awards ceremony, the Nitty Gritty Dirt Band played a cover of "Will the Circle Be Unbroken," with a wide variety of new and old pickers—making a clear argument that they were the tradition and that their cohort, for example, New Grass Revival, belonged on the same stage as The Carter Sisters or Roy Acuff. Dolly was in the room that night, and her voice appears in the concert, but she is not shown on camera and doesn't get a solo. Dolly shows up in a repeat from a 1988 segment, where she is flirting with Randy Travis, and in 1989, they share a quick joke. Travis feels slightly embarrassed by the attention—turning the tables on the kind of putting people into place that Carson did.

In a year where she had an album and a movie to promote, Dolly is not very visible, sliding behind these neo-traditionalists. There is some message in who gets a solo in the Dirt Band, an act of canon making, because the song was mega-traditional—the thing about an unbroken circle is that some people are always in it and some people are always out of it—in this presentation, one of the founders of modern country and one of the best ambassadors of the genre had a reputation that was so gigantic that she could not have been ignored entirely, but she was not in that circle; on that stage, on that moment, her placement was outside the central circle.

In this space, it might be useful to consider exactly what the traditionalism of neo-traditionalism considers—specifically noting albums.

1989 was not a year of radical reinvention for country music, but the significance was clear in that the neo-traditionalist movement of the mid-1980s had finally settled—becoming the dominant mode and proving that mode had significant staying power. This mode was marked by a complex sentimentality, foregrounding a cishet masculinity; its tradition did not consider the dense and lush production before it or even the faux roughness of the outlaws. That said, it was also a significant year for Parton, her performance in *Steel Magnolias* had Oscar buzz, and her role as Truvy Jones, while not a stretch, was her best-acted screen role, perhaps ever. Also, in interviews for *TNT*, and in the press releases sent out, she was as concerned about the opening of Dollywood as she was about the movie or the album. Both movies and music were in the mix, but felt on the edge of it. (Really in theme park design too, more Knott's Berry Farm than Disney.)

Neo-traditionalist commitment to a kind of male family ignored Dolly's domesticity. This movement was mostly about the stories of men. They sang about commitment, about desire, or about love—but the messages, often beautiful, sometimes wry, or funny, were less vexed than Parton. There was an unfortunate revival here, where Parton did not make a traditionalist album as an entire collection of men who were more committed to the bit and were rewarded for their commitment. *White Limozeen* sold, but it did not sound as new as the boys who were doing old-fashioned things. The exception might have been Reba, whose voice, twang, and domestic melodramas were establishing a similar relationship between person and personae. This neo-traditionalism feels like a summing-up of a decade whose formal and informal politics were less about pleasure and more about policing bodies and their relationships. For all of its gorgeousness, there was nothing more reactionary than Travis' "Deeper than a Holler," for example, an ode to straight men loving straight women, with vocals that underlined its current of biological essentialism.

There is an exception that can be seen with Reba McEntire, who had substantial success at this time. If she was considered to be neo-traditonalist, it was her unreconstituted Oklahoma accent. I think she sounded that way sometimes—not outside of the radio with Travis, for example, but her concerns were startlingly modern, and her ennui was not related to the past at all—for example, she wrote "She Thinks His Name Was John," Nashville's first real AIDS song (not a good AIDS song), and wrote as much of the suburbs as she did of the mythic west.

Reba wrote a great album, moving between the pop and the neo-traditionalist instincts, more expansive, more lustful, and less sentimental, but it occurred in 1990's *Rumor Has It*. The album is sumptuous, indulgent, and heartbreaking—it has the writerly details of heartbreak that "The Moon, the Stars, and Me" fails to achieve—see, for example, how she sings "Rumor" on the breakout single "Rumor Has It," but it was written by Bruce Burch, Vern Dant, and Larry Shell—Reba is one of country's interpretive singers, but she is less of a writer. (See also the twang on "You Lie," another song written by others but owned by Reba—and perhaps one of the last great examples of the old Nashville tradition of recording a cover soon after an initial recording and making it definitive—it was first recorded by Cee Cee Chapman, a performer whose career started blazing in 1988 and was mostly over by 1993.)

The song that had the most cultural impact on Nashville, and seemed to be a direct rejoinder of the ambivalence of *White Limozeen*, or it would have been, if Bobby Gentry didn't record it in 1969 or Irma Thomas didn't try it in the early 1970s. Gentry wrote the record, and Thomas' work survived on bootlegs until an official reissue was released about a decade ago. Reba's version of "Fancy" sounds like an extended, deepened, pedal steel-laden reworking of the Southern gothic original. A tale of a Southern woman who is turned out by her mother and who succeeds as a sex worker so well that she is given real estate in New York and LA. Dolly plays at being a sex worker, or a madam, but she rarely places herself as someone who sells sex for money herself—the song sounds like it could be on one of those neo-traditional records and is a result of a close reading of a country tradition.

The amorality of "Fancy" and the morality of "White Limozeen" (the song) provide two ways of working through a tradition, but listening to other albums of the 1989–1990 year, a year dominated by men's voices and men's understanding of country music, is different.

*White Limozeen* landed in one of Nashville's perpetual gender wars, where an emerging canon of these traditionalists excluded women. Though they often wrote about women abstractly, throughout the 1980s, this cluster of performers was gelling, working through the same themes, the same sounds, and often the same gender. Their presence in Nashville meant it was fairly rare for women's voices to succeed—Reba being a more obvious example than Dolly, not an upstart, *Rumor Has It* was her fifteenth album, and she would eventually follow Parton's example—with successful film, stage, and television career—perhaps more successful than Dolly, playing Annie Oakley on Broadway and having a sitcom which lasted more than a few seasons.

In 1989, though, the men still ruled, and 1989's albums followed the overwhelming conservatism of the previous decade. I am thinking of Clint Black's *Killin' Time*, George Strait's *Beyond the Blue Neon*, Nitty Gritty Dirt Band's *Will*

*The Circle Be Unbroken,* and a dry, ironic, cousin—Lyle Lovett's *Lyle Lovett and His Large Band.*

Each of these albums was both a cultural and commercial success, shifting how the genre was viewed and leading to a boom unseen since the Urban Cowboy boom a decade earlier. Listening to them made one aware of how slightly out of fashion *White Limozeen* sounded, and the struggles with how an album sounded or what it meant could be solved by the complete forgoing of the pop/country dialectic or even the hee haw dialectic, which was Dolly's central crisis. Considering them against *White Limozeen* provides a lens for the ongoing crisis of representation in Nashville.

*Killin' Time* is a good representation of this battling of genre and tradition. It sold very well, eventually going triple platinum, and it picked up an audience that recognized the necessity of putting the new in traditionalism. This traditionalism included love songs, breaking up songs, drinking songs, and songs that shuffled those themes with an elegant exactitude. None of the themes were new, and few of them were clever, but the almost slickness of the production refuses any ambivalence. Dolly's songs from 1989, though they have an edge of hesitance, have an ironic distance between presentation and quality; something that's absent here. The first track on *Killin' Time*, "Straight from the Factory," is a full commitment to western swing—it might be the most complex—a swing song about monogamy—a song about factory work which argues against the kind of endless reputation of similar objects which factories encourage. There might be a pun there; Randy Lewis of the Los Angeles Times suggests that Black might be quoting Strait: "musically he can Western-swing just as hard as fellow Texan George Strait, which he proves on the delightful 'Straight From the Factory."

If it's a pun, it's a bad one, and it lacks the density of signifiers that exist in the best of Parton's writing—when he says, in the song, that his lover is ". . .the only lock that's made to fit my key"—it's not a new line, it has been used in Hamlet, and it has been used by Bessie Smith—but both with more hunger or more vulgarity than the polite, technically well accomplished, beautiful work that Black provides here. The rest of the album features well-constructed tropes without much risk of excess—I believe in Dolly's lust when she sings "why'd you come in here lookin like that," and though Black's "Walkin' Away" talks about "[His] finest hour spent here with you in the dark," the melancholy is there, but the lust isn't. There was a current of lust in Dolly's best work, or if not lust, then desire, which she hungered for. Her best work rests on the tension between the hunger satiated or not— hunger widely defined. For Dolly, the hunger was traditional, starting perhaps with food but very much about sex. Though Clint Black and George Strait were marketed as sex objects, even when the metaphors are so phallic or explicit, like the aforementioned lock and key, they lack the liquid flowing between wanting and receiving that marks Dolly's best work, even on *White Limozeen* with its songs about big cities, country heartbreak, and Jesus Christ.

It's a marvel that the label let *White Limozeen* be as lusty as it is. There is nothing courtly, nothing shameful, about Dolly's "Wait 'Til I Get You Home," you know exactly what the singer and her male companion are going to do when they get home, and that they want to do in private is easily forecast by what they are doing in public—plus it quotes "Behind Closed Doors," perhaps the horniest song of the 70s. The song is doubly horny, conceptually committed to the horn. Rich has the courtly distance, the wink, and the nod that the neo-traditionalists are playing. Dolly is making a slight joke about Rich's public/private distinctions in ways that the neo-trads never quite manage. If Black is making formally retrograde, well-constructed, and elegant music, which provides a distance from his feelings, he does not integrate them as effectively as Parton does, and it's not nearly as lusty as the strings in Rich's hit.

I think about the 1989 CMA Awards, thinking about who got their shine and who didn't, who was there and who was absent, and realizing that not only Dolly was missing in that circle but also Tammy Wynette and Loretta Lynn. I wonder if the country music circle is always broken and always being reassembled a Ship of Theseus of creation and recreation, and a polite fiction that who is in and out of the circle is forever—a place can be found permanently within it if someone is good enough for long enough. Placing *White Limozeen* within its 1989 context, that is proven not to be the case.

# 8
# Anointed

At the 1990 Gospel Music Awards, Dolly Parton sang the contemporary worship song "He's Alive," with a 100-person choir. Dolly has never really done 'austere,' but figuring out exactly how she sings this complex song is a good indication of how Dolly has aestheticized other, more austere versions—a key to Dolly's performance overall. "He's Alive" is a story song told from the perspective of Peter on the night of Christ's crucifixion. The first four verses narrate the crucifixion as almost a domestic melodrama. She sings it acapella, holding onto every edge of suspense. If you are Christian (and possibly even if you aren't), you know the story, and it is a miracle that anyone can get any suspense out of it at all.

Parton tells the story via small details, a rigid guitar, and the quietness of her voice, working the tension of the verses:

And half in fear the day
Would find the soldiers breakin' through
To drag us all away
And just before the sunrise

I heard something at the wall
The gate began to rattle
And a voice began to call

The song then explodes open, and a hundred robed choir members descend from the wings, boosting up Dolly's voice—the joy of the resurrection matched by the lush exuberance of the singing. It isn't that Dolly cannot care about the gothic or the violent—some of her best work explores where the domestic falls into the abject, and some of the her best story songs are ones where, for example, children are in peril (the two major ones being "Me and Little Andy" and "Applejack"). The first half of the song "He's Alive" is very much in that vein. But the song ends with hope—there is an optimistic quality, where "Heaven's gates are open wide."

She performed it at the Dove Awards for the American Gospel Association because it was a single from *White Limozeen*. The song is a simulacrum of a nineteenth-century storytelling song written by an evangelical preacher named Don Francisco in 1977 and recorded by Johnny Cash in 1979. To understand Parton's work on this track, one has to think of her own Pentecostal upbringing, her commercial instincts, her skills as an interpretative singer, the nature of the song itself, and how it works as a recording versus a live performance. Notice how she combines the secular and the sacred, and how she elides the tension between those two forms in her specific space and time.

Don Francisco, one of the earliest of the 1970s musicians who created the genre of contemporary Christian music, was a complex figure, not having the strangeness of Larry Norman or the slickness of someone like Chris Tomlin. Beginning from the folk revival of the 1960s and 1970s his work has a painful earnestness. He doesn't seduce with flash or bang but moves with something smaller and plainer. Parton is capable of the plainness, but the push of this, the excess of it, slides into the rest of the album—over the top, lush, and deeply committed to the body.

Francisco's song begins with a single strum of a guitar, and there is a long guitar section before he starts talking. He doesn't quite talk though—this is a sermon song, sort of like a story song, spoken as much as it is sung. He runs on the dramatic potential of the work, and overemphasizes some words, but those words are ones that are emphasized in many Easter liturgies. Though there is a definitive, dramatic narrative, and though the song speeds up as Magdalene finds the empty tomb, it doesn't quite have the heft or gravitas of Dolly at her best.

There is also a coda at the end—after the song discusses the betrayal of Peter—where the song moves from the very local context of first-century Palestine to a canonically understood Messiah outside of space and time considered timeless. It is not quite the same coda as Dolly, though one can see the seed of the idea in the shift between the verseless story structure and the ending of the resurrection. The *Encyclopedia of Christian Contemporary Music* describes the song as one where "piano chords crash into the song, utterly destroying its structure and replacing the loping melody with a bombastic chorus."

The bombast is still slightly restrained on Don Francisco's version, there is little ecstasy in how he sings the last word, "hallelujah." The song rests on the balance between the grim threat of death and torture in the storytelling section and the rupture of the hallelujah. The song concentrates much more on the 'hallelujah' and spends much less time on the abject.

There are other versions before Dolly's version, but the most significant one might be from Johnny Cash's double album, 1979's *A Believer Sings the Truth*. Cash, at his worst, is overwrought. He is not a subtle performer, and it seems like when he believes in his material, he becomes less and less subtle. This is the least tennous of the popular versions. It features the Tennessee Two and a chugging guitar line, a looped vocal when he talks about dying, two gospel choruses (including one in the middle of the song, which keens), June Carter Cash playing Magdalene, and funhouse organs—all before the "he's alive" portion starts. It's country at its most overgilded.

The Francisco and Cash versions suggested a successful way forward. Francisco was hyper-aware of the song's success—both critically and commercially. The *Encyclopedia of Contemporary Christian Music* writes, "Cashbox magazine called the song 'one of the best folk gospel ballads of all time.'" More than twenty years after its release, a bevy of critics selected it as one of CCM's top 10 best songs in the history of contemporary Christian music. The song remains tied with Dallas Holm's "Rise Again" as the longest-running chart single in the history of Christian radio.

The song is so successful—regardless of how it's recorded, with the folk spareness of Francisco, the overly baroque production of Cash, or the sudden ascension of Dolly—because of how it's structured. You have to know the Bible pretty well in order to understand the first minute or so of the song, but it resembles the moral storytelling popular at the time—something close to "Ghost Riders in the Sky," or "Twenty-Five Minutes to Go."

Though there is no singular American Christianity, it might be useful to think of how Dolly sanctified this as her own kind of religious history. There is little doubt that Dolly has been saved. Her daddy preached and wrote albums. She has talked in interviews often about going to a little country church on Sunday. She ended up in a Pentecostal church, and though it might have been a way of teasing city folks, has claimed to have snake-handling cousins. Pentecostal music undulates on exhaled and inhaled breath, risking losing control or being overtaken. Named after the Pentecost, or the miracle where the holy spirit takes control over an early church congregation, it is a durational performance of it's own holiness.

Dolly's religious music and her hymn singing are quite conventional. Though she sings gospel songs, they are songs that could be marked by both her figure resting at the front of a concert hall instead of a church and by her own control. Parton is not reckless with her instrument, and even on live performances, her band is so tight that it mirrors the sheen of the recording studio.

Dolly's recording of "He's Alive," as closing song on an album that was supposed to renovate her career, is on the edge of excess. It leans on the final chorus with its belief in the written Christ and that chorus rises and floats seemingly endlessly, though well controlled. The coda is one of the spaces where Dolly moves out of the way. The song being taken over by a chorus is explicitly collective in a way that is different from the duets or the tight bands—it is not Dolly controlling, but Dolly giving up her voice—a point made more explicit by the size and scale of the gospel choir at the Dove Awards.

The church too can always be considered as a collective whole, though there are often soloists and special musical numbers. A song belongs to the story of Christ; the importance of telling the story of Christ is not necessarily to boost the ego of a performer but to save souls. For example, what money Francisco made from his version was returned back to the church; Cash's label, Columbia, did not think his gospel album would sell in any significant numbers, so it was released on his own private label—as much of a tool of evangelism as a new album from the man in black.

The 1900 Dove Award celebration marked a shift in Christian aesthetics. There has always been excess in American Christian aesthetics, and they have always been quick to use new technologies—the tent revivals in the 1890s, or the radio sermons of the 1930s. It also adapted to technology very early—some of the earliest TV shows were Christian shows, and there has been a robust cross-denominational film industry for as long as film has existed. "He's Alive" comes from the Jesus People movement, which evangelized using the post-hippie craving for events and happenings. But the excess of the gospel genre, how it used the same kind of tragedy of Southern womanhood, and high femme aesthetics to convince, sometimes using music, was relatively new. Throughout the 1970s and 1980s, a second generation of mass media preachers, after the radio preachers from the 1920s to the 1940s showed up on trans-continental broadcasts in the same kind of aesthetic that Dolly had been selling for years. But they were less in control of their material and aesthetic than she is, and their performances slid unintentionally into camp. Watching this Dove Award performance is a pointed rejoinder to Tammy Faye Bakker or Jan Crouch. Dolly comes out from among these angels, and the shot tightens on her. The focus is on as much of Dolly—childless Dolly, decadent Dolly, Dolly who moved to Babylon—as it was on Christ, as a kind of seeking of forgiveness. A meta performance, finally converging the spirits of Jimmy Swaggart and his cousin Jerry Lee Lewis.

There is Gospel and there is gospel, and Dolly has always played between those lines—maybe the easiest definition is that Gospel is intended explicitly for religious spaces, it's liturgical music, work that fits into the ebb and flow of a service, while gospel is the genre, which sounds like church music but can fit into secular recording studios, concert halls, and even arenas. Like most traditions in America, it has a complex history of borrowing, segregation, bodily intervention, and coy refusals. Most of all, it's a form. When Ed Ochs asked the Gospel musician and Aretha Franklin intimate James Cleveland what Gospel was in a 1980 interview for Billboard, he responded: "Gospel singing is the counterpart of gospel teaching, so we'd like to have that uppermost in their minds; that it's an art form, true enough, but it represents an idea, a thought, a trend.

It must be, then in some sense—have a pragmatic and explicit use need."

When Dolly sings "He's Alive," the first thing that the listener has to keep in mind is that she is making an argument for the physical resurrection of Jesus Christ after being crucified and after being in the tomb for three days. She is also arguing that the only way that the audience can also be alive in the love of God is through asking Christ, who sacrificed himself to save people, to do that saving.

She is taking the argument the late 1970s post-denominational Jesus People movement made and translating it into her own Pentecostalism. The denominational mode is strong here, though the producer, Skaggs was Baptist, as was Cash, whose cover popularized the song.

Dolly has mentioned in interviews with Christian media that in her Pentecostal youth, she was considered "anointed." There is an idea in Pentecostal circles that one is taken over by God, that the singing or dancing or movement involves some autonomy, but is mostly sacred forces assuming will over the body, and by extension, the work coming from that body. In his brilliant book, *Blackpentecostal Breath*, Ashon Crawley works out exactly how Pentecostalism might provide a new understanding of Dolly singing a song like "He's Alive"— namely, that "performance constitutes a tradition" (8), so not only is the Pentecostal church told via scripture, but through a set of performances and memories of performances. I would argue that Parton's singing enacts her Southerness, when she breaks into syllabics, when she rises high into an almost falsetto, when she does the call and response, throughout her career, and on this song specifically, she is working through a performance tradition, one that draws not only on growing up in and singing in church in Tennesse, but on familial religious tradition. For how singular Dolly is, the familial tradition is one kind of performance–but her breaking out of the communal quality of her family is a break out of the gospel tension.

Crawley continues: "something is there, in the aesthetic practices, aesthetic practices that are collective intellectual performances, that serve as antagonistic to the very doctrines of sin and flesh that so proliferate within the world" (24). The aesthetic connection here is not the explicit logophilia of the bible, of the reading and writing of the scripture, but of the performance, the oral tradition of preaching and hymn singing—a preaching and hymn singing, a collectivism that could be considered restricted or small. Dolly talks about how she had to learn how to be Christian in *her* way, and perhaps not even Christian, when she talks about how limiting the tradition and the aesthetic practices. It is a kind of doubling or mirroring, to enter the world of sin and pleasure. She has to understand that the pleasures of Pentecostal singing brought her in one direction, but that direction might not be exactly where she wanted to land. In her autobiography, *Dolly,* from 1997, she tells one story about that:

I also felt that they had misinterpreted the words "God-fearing." Maybe this was because the Bible had been translated from Hebrew. Maybe it was because many of the people passing on the word of God couldn't read or write. They were limited by what they were told was truth by other illiterate people, who had been told it by others, and so on.

"He's Alive" is a summing up of the albums and sounds differently than Parton's other forays into gospel. It also sounds different than Johnny Cash. The exuberance of the song, the raucous quality of the instrumentation, suggests the kind of performance at home, but it also has flash, a kind of overwhelming kitsch, an idea or an imagining of what losing one's control for Christ would mean, instead of the actual love of Christ—though the love of Christ must be serious. The collectivism becomes her as a leader, perhaps a burlesque of her grandfather's charismatic preaching, perhaps a commitment to all-American devotion as a spectacle for spectacle's sake— somewhere between Aimee Semple MacPherson and the late Elvis, singing the American Trilogy, his sweat-drenched handkerchiefs offered to an audience like relics.

The song does not mention Christ or Peter or Magdalene by name. The narrative rests on knowing the history without naming them—the obliqueness of this not naming darkens and tightens a narrative—like entering into that tomb with Christ, and then the blast of the coda, like the lightness of the stone being rolled away. The form of the song matches the content—and this tight loop of the story being told, and how the story is being told, has an interior elegance. It is intended for insiders.

Insiders being American Christians resting on both the Word and vernacular depictions of that Gospel. This is how Dolly absorbs the text, how she makes it her own. Though Dolly is known to be a songwriter, and thus more often borrowed from than borrower, she understands both hymn singing and country music—that the genre rests on taking, improving, and giving back. The idea of authorship is fairly loose, and especially as seen in albums from the 1960s and 1970s—a song would be written, then recorded, it would be heard, recorded again, and all of these versions would sell. People would be interested in how different artists would interpret a work.

The presence of a church song on a comeback album has a little bit of a cynical edge. Parton is so often thought to now as a secular saint, and there is less and less of a consideration today that she could do work for money. But this song had moved relatively quickly from a song beloved by Christians to one that had entered a canon of worship music. So Dolly's recording of this song, more than a decade after Cash and the original, was not an effort to promote an unknown artist but to absorb their success. It's not that she didn't believe in the material, that her faith was not an explicit part of her interest in the work—but that the commercial and the pious are intermingled. There are few vows of poverty in American Christianity.

# Conclusion

Often 33 1/3 volumes are products of enthusiasms—complex enthusiasms but ones that assume that the album is both canonical and good, perhaps making the slight mistake that they are canonical because they are good. An act of unmitigated fandom does not have to be absent of critical rigor. I'm thinking, for example, of Annie Zaleski's brilliant book on *Rio* by Duran Duran. Reading that work made me reconsider a band I thought was frivolous; Zaleski's passionate zeal converted me. There are also moments where the writing is so complex and so beautiful, and I cannot understand why the appeal of the album, even with fandom, exists; I will never understand exactly what people see in Neutral Milk Hotel, and I am not enough of a gearhead to appreciate the complex musicology of Radiohead, no matter how much Dai Griffiths's careful commitment to *OK Computer's* formalism. Even when the series gets weird, like the word games of the Magnetic Fields book or John Darnielle's novella about Sabbath.

There has been so much written about her and by her, and so there was also some anxiety about starting a Dolly book about, what else could be said, and what needs to be said by me. Or, to put it another way, a critic's role is to write not about what they love, necessarily, but about what they find interesting. Dolly is endlessly interesting, writing about Dolly is rarely boring, and writing about any album must also reflect in how she constructed herself, the construction of the persona of Dolly, her great work, a scaffolding for any music that occurs. That was where I started with the book—I thought that the series had a gap in country music (at my pitching, there were only five or so books that covered the whole genre, and none of them were really populist); the biggest gap in the series country writing, for me, seemed to be Dolly.

I knew that I wanted to write about her career, her process, and her life, and I narrowed it down to a few albums that did that well—1973's *My Tennessee Mountain Home* or 1993's *The Grass is Blue*, or maybe *Rainbow*. They all had some things in common: they had a distinct point of view; they allowed me to write about tradition, desire, and personae; and they were albums that marked transitions in her life and career: her break with Porter Wagoner, her careful return to tradition after decades of anxiety about genre, her pop turns.

The transitions and the turns for Dolly, in these albums, reflected two central issues in her career—the first is the dialectic between authenticity and performance; the second is the move between the small/local and the globally famous. Thinking about those two problems, plus the questions of geography, how that interacted with genre, and her own iconic status, the album that seemed to be the closest to reflect those issues was *White Limozeen*. Considering the history of the series, it seemed cold, maybe a little too analytical, to consider writing about Dolly not as a fan but as an example of the crisis of taste—to use the album as a lens to reflect a larger history of her career and her fandom.

I hope that I have not done a disservice to Dolly. But I also think that it is a disservice to treat an artist only as good—as a saint, as morally uncomplicated, as musically interesting at all times. There is so much written about Dolly as genius, as brilliant musician, and so much of that seems to be inarguable. (Though there is still a bit of class and gender bias—she is as good or better a songwriter than the cluster of 1970s male singer-songwriters—as good as Dylan, for example, and she doesn't have the Nobel.) The shift of criticism in this digital age to a kind of accelerated fandom means that there is social pressure to oversimplify artists' career—to flatten the complexity and depth.

I have been thinking about this kind of flattening, and thinking about how ubiquitous the love for Dolly is and about how it seems to be impossible to complicate—that to notice that she might have difficulty with race, or that she might be deeply committed to capitalism, or that her friendship with queerness might be conditional, or that her wit separates herself from true solidarity with the working poor, or other levels on which she has not always acted the ways we might wish. I've been thinking that Dolly's genius was her ability to be all things to everyone, and that what *White Limozeen* was, was an interesting failure. An interesting failure, which showed the edges of taste, the mechanics behind her ambition, and exactly where her record label or her audience allowed her to go.

In his book about Celine Dion, Carl Wilson writes about the democratization of taste—and about what it means to collapse the boundaries between fan and artist:

> This is what I mean by democracy—not a limp open-mindedness, but actively grappling with people and things not like me, which brings with it the perilous question of what I am like. Democracy, that dangerous, paradoxical and mostly unattempted ideal, sees that the self is insufficient, dependent for definition on otherness, and chooses not only to accept that but to celebrate it, to stake everything on it.

When Dolly is like all things to all people, when her ubiquity is thought to be democratic, the grappling does not occur. Assuming that Dolly is for all of us does not allow us to recognize that she is working through a very specific milieu and does not then make complex our own relationships to class or race (on a personal level, for example—seeing her as just a gay icon does not allow a full examination of her work with someone like Kid Rock; seeing her as someone who climbed from poverty conflates my own lower-middle-class existence with her grinding poverty). Dolly, on this record, is one who is uniquely positioned. It comes from the South, from harshness, from the church. Its uniqueness is what to celebrate, in its raggedness, its strangeness, and in its anxiety and desperation. She stakes her own career on it—a career that allowed for another kind of democracy to emerge.

Dolly's democratic instinct, then, is more often found in the liminal failures than in the ubiquitous, sing-along singles—regardless of how genius "9–5" or "Jolene" are.

# Coda

I wrote and edited parts of this book, on a three-week trip through the South, selling my previous book on Tammy Wynette. I was in North Carolina and Tennessee. In that time, I saw Dollywood on billboards throughout Asheville and Durham/Chapel Hill. I saw her visage on t-shirts at Berks Department Store, and Dillards, at the Cracker Barrel near Tunnel Road, and on people of all genders walking through the streets of Asheville. I even saw a little collection of Parton books in the mall's Barnes and Noble. When I got to Nashville, I saw all of the t-shirts, posters, prints, and tchotchkes in the souvenir shops and candy stores of the tourist mecca of lower Broadway, in the midst of blaring neon for Blake Shelton and Kid Rock. I saw t-shirts for sale saying 'What Would Dolly Do,' a post-Christian, Deep South idolatry; I saw the same message on similar gear in the East Nashville hipster record store Grimeys (though the only Dolly records I saw at Grimeys were the expensive reissues of *Jolene* and the 180 gram versions of her latest work with Patterson). I saw expensive coffee table editions, at sixty or seventy dollars, of *Storyteller*. I didn't see, in the used bookstores or the new bookstores, copies of Sarah

Smarsh's clever and well-articulated memoir *She Come By It Natural: Dolly Parton and the Women Who Lived Her Songs* or Lynn Melnick's poetic, difficult blending of memoir and analysis, *I've Had to Think Up a Way to Survive: On Trauma, Persistence, and Dolly Parton.*

I spent twelve hours over two days at the Country Music Hall of Fame Archives, and looking over my right shoulder were two faux-naive postcards, little icons—one of Dolly and one of Loretta; on the desk of the archivist was a photo of Dolly and the archivist's stepfather in a studio in the 1970s. When I finished at the archives, I went back to my hotel, which was pricey, new, and a total temple to Dolly's image as ironic kitsch savior. The hotel was part of the chain called the Graduate and was within walking distance of lower Broadway. Seeming to cater to bachelorette parties, the experience was a location where what was traditionally considered genteel good taste (chintz, Victorian botanical illustrations, white marble) was enfolded gently into what was traditionally considered bad taste (the giant neon gas station sign inside). The vulgar product was tatted and airbrushed so that fun became "fun"—you could see this in the taco bar, called "Cross Eyed Critters Watering Hole," hidden on the first floor, with its velvet paintings of country royalty and an animatronic band. This was a riff on and return to the South, against Disney's attempt to do something similar in the 1970s (The Country Bear Jamboree), but an ironic gesture of an infantilized remake of Southern culture that may not be very respectful.

In front of the elevators, two George Condo-style paintings of Dolly, with her face fractured, opening up to reveal a crude cartoon of Mickey Mouse—again a clever idea but an idea that seems ambivalent, one of which could be insulting, and one whose gag depends on the violent dissolution of Dolly's image; a tribute that, on reflection, doesn't appear to like its subject very much. The carpets to get to the hotel room were soothing pinks and grays, again in a tasteful pattern. Genteel. Some of the furniture would not have been out of place in any upper-middle-class living room—a midnight blue velvet couch with a scalloped back, a pastel Oriental-style area rug, and an occasional chair upholstered in blue-and-white-striped seersucker. Some of the design elements resembled the kitsch downstairs—the wallpaper throughout, with its wide cream and pink stripes, the stripes the color of dental fluoride, or the strawberry ice cream available in four-liter buckets at the discount supermarkets. The brass squirrel figurine. She is photographed at Studio 54 with Bianca Jagger's horse.

Sometimes there was something that was beyond taste (the room, of course, but also maybe how Dolly isn't camp). The bed. Four-poster, with a careful canopy created from an elaborate floral damask. Between the headboard and behind the damask was a curtain of red and white seersucker. Floating on that curtain of seersucker is a painting of Dolly. I say a painting, but it's most likely a transfer on rough canvas, something that someone could have bought from Sears and Roebuck catalogs as decoration for a rec room. Again, Dolly is an example to be lauded and a kitsch joke to be mocked—her high femme qualities mocked—nothing more important than that anonymous girl riding, or the brass squirrel, or like downstairs an entertainment like the pinball machine and the animatronic bear being the same kind of entertainment. I recognize my tastes run low, and my critical lens runs toward collapsing entertainments and genres, so the pleasure of excess was not the problem, as much as the quality.

This continued onto the rooftop bar. The bar was art-directed, within an inch of its life, into three sections—the outdoor patio, the inside bar, and a living-room parlor section. Coming out of the elevator, there was a life-sized airbrushed portrait of Dolly, the same style that was selling burlesque dancers in Printer's Alley—there was a kind of clever allusion there. The bar was giant, shining formica, and the collection of high tables around it were too close together. The menu had cocktails that sounded good but were badly balanced. The food was vaguely French, with only the desserts playing at kitsch. It's strange to eat a mediocre chicken dish, dated and not revived, and drinking an okay but not great glass of white wine, while staring at a pool where people's fun was heavily mediated by both location and place. The living-room area had more velvet portraits, this time three-quarters and of women—only one Black, the only Black representation of Southern culture I saw in the whole place. They used the same brass floor lamps, the same Polo Lounge palm wallpaper, and the same tile that I have seen in places that were more expensive than fun in Toronto or Chicago or New York. I wondered, with Dolly's cooking shows, her cookbooks, and her commitment to Southern food, with decades of reclaiming poor Southern food for rich peoples, about two hundred dollar a person dinners that I have eaten or read about in Savannah or Charleston or New Orleans, why there was no attempt to craft a menu around Dolly's idea of the south. Even the music was mostly 1980s pop hits—you were more likely to hear Madonna than "9–5."

This motif of Dolly as Instagram story or the idea of Dolly rather than Dolly as person or creator or writer reached its nadir on the too-small patio, with a plunge pool, five or six giant raspberry-colored umbrellas shading white plastic loungers, and overlooking all of this a monumental statue of Dolly's head, made of pink fiberglass, and looking like it was carved out of scrapple. The bar White Limozeen was a mash-up of tourist aesthetics, a baroque far past distinctions of taste, past music-making.

The bar is a true extension of the album. Consider it the point where Dolly's aesthetics shifted, perhaps even becoming a loss leader instead of an actual album, one product among a dozen or more commercial potentials, the larger consequence of a capitalism which precludes a carefully curated ahistorical aesthetic. All of that said, people seemed to have a good time.

# Acknowledgments

For my mother, who taught me both about gender and country music but also how to read and how to consider complex ideas.

For Ben and Carl, again first and best readers.

For Mariead, for being an early and astute reader.

For my Hamilton crew, who made a place seem real— Aaron, Alex, Ashley, Ben N., Brandon, Cath, Charles, Danica, Gary, Jamie, Josh M., Rob, Sonali, T, Tara.

(Also for Printed Word, King West Books, Epic, and City and the City)

For Josh, who makes me reconsider complex landscapes, even when the Woodman's has lost its luster. And for Thomas, for explaining Indiana as a place and an idea of a place.

For the country massive, who is changing how we consider country music, and calls bullshit/checks facts and feelings: (Ann, Amanda, Barry, Charles, David, Francesca, Jewly, Joey, Justin, Marissa, Nathalie).

Alfred, Chris M., Jamie T., Jody, Karen, Keith, Matos, Marissa, Nate, Nathalie, Sarah, and Stuart the solidarity of labor, that is writing, in this age indifferent to labor.

For Kristy, Lucas, and Martin—whose queerness is open and expansive, and makes me feel hope in an age of encroaching fascism.

For Graham and Mack, who still are excellent at explaining the social politics of the West.

For Sarah, who edited this, and Leah, who commissioned it.

And of course:

D, Patrick, Raymond, decades into the struggle. Kathleen Campbell at the Country Music Hall of Fame.

# Works Cited

July 25, 1977. Mac Davis / Dolly Parton at Painters Mill Music Fair Owings Mills, Maryland, United States | Concert Archives.

December 21, 1979. Mac Davis: A Christmas Special, NBC. https://www.youtube.com/watch?v=KSYeD7x_X3c.

Academy of Country Music | Search Winners. n.d. https://www.acmcountry.com/winners?awardTitle=Dolly+Parton&awardCategory=&awardYear=&actionButton=Submitl.

Access Hollywood. 2023. "Dolly Parton Jokes about Having a 'Threesome' w/ Garth Brooks & Trisha Yearwood." *YouTube*, May 12. https://www.youtube.com/watch?v=E8z5LTzLLA4.

Anderson, Caryss. 2023. June. https://consequence.net/2023/05/dolly-parton-declined-presidential-medal-of-freedom/.

Art Gallery of Ontario. https://ago.ca/exhibitions/andy-warhol.

Batteau, Allen. 1979. "Appalachia and the Concept of Culture: A Theory of Shared Misunderstandings." *Appalachian Journal* 7, no. 1/2: 9–31. http://www.jstor.org/stable/40932719.

Beghtol, L.D. 2006. *69 Love Songs: A Field Guide*. New York: Continuum.

Billboard. n.d. "Dolly Parton." https://www.billboard.com/artist/dolly-parton/chart-history/hsi/.

Black, Clint. 1989. *Killin' Time*. Nashville: RCA.

BubbleUp LTD. n.d. *Benghazi Ain't Going Away*. The Charlie Daniels Band. https://www.charliedaniels.com/soap-box?b_id=5670.

Capp Al Frank, Frazetta, and Denis Kitchen. 2003. *Li'l Abner : The Frazetta Years*. 1st ed. Milwaukie, OR: Dark Horse Comics.

Cash, Johnny. 1965. "25 Minutes to Go." *Johnny Cash Sings the Songs of the True West*. Columbia.

Cecelia, Conway. 1995. *African Banjo Echoes in Appalachia: A Study of Folk Traditions*. 1st ed. Knoxville: University of Tennessee Press.

Christgau, Robert, and White Limozeen. 1989. https://www.robertchristgau.com/get_album.php?id=5794.

"1989 CMA Will the Circle Be Unbroken." [Video]. *YouTube*. https://www.youtube.com/watch?v=gUI8l0QChh4.

Cottom, Terri. "The Dolly Moment." https://tressie.substack.com/p/the-dolly-moment.

Country Music Assoc. https://cmaawards.com/past-winners-and-nominees/?appSession=41G9LK34CF81O9I7I4Q0H48843Q2048CFH3M97Q20BISD1E98EZRK9W7YW1DV305E1R12J314UFAAB7F014017H2L9UCPRVV90NA59YG2KGV79P4Y2BPQ92B54GF5F6C&RecordID=&PageID=2&PrevPageID=2&cbNewPageSize=50.

Country Music Assoc. Awards Ceremony. 1980. https://www.youtube.com/watch?v=33GyphBCkXY.

Country Music Songwriters Hall of Fame. Mac Davis. ttps://nashvillesongwritersfoundation.com/Site/inductee?entry_id=1495.

Clark, Bob. 1984. *Rhinestone*. 20th Century Fox.

CNN. https://www.cnn.com/2020/12/01/entertainment/barack-obama-dolly-parton/index.html.

Crawley Ashon, T. 2017. *Blackpentecostal Breath: The Aesthetics of Possibility*. Version 1st ed. New York: Fordham University Press. http://english.digitaliapublishing.com/a/69194/.

Cusic, Don. 2010. *Encyclopedia of Contemporary Christian Music: Pop Rock and Worship*. Santa Barbara Calif: Greenwood Press. http://ebooks.abc-clio.com/?isbn=9780313344268.

Darnielle, John. 2008. *Black Sabbath's Master of Reality: Master of Reality*. London: Continuum International Pub.

Discogs. White Limozeen. https://www.discogs.com/release /2893251-Dolly-Parton-White-Limozeen.

"Dolly, Embarrasses Randy Travis, at the 1989 23rd Annual Country Music Awards." [Video]. *YouTube*. https://www .youtube.com/watch?v=HnSJnDhiWM4 the 1988 segment was rebroadcast in the 1989 one.

"Dolly Parton 'He's Alive' 21st Annual Dove Awards 1990 | An." n.d. https://www.facebook.com/watch/?v=1428754720913122.

Elving, R. 2022. "How Loretta Lynn, Country Music and a Rural Republican Tide Changed U.S. Politics." *NPR*, October 8. https://www.npr.org/2022/10/08/1127230406/loretta-lynn -country-music-politics-republicans.

Flatt and Scruggs. 1974. "Live Recordings 1950–1960." *Vintage Recordings*.

Flat, Scruggs and the Foggy Mountain Boys. 1950. *Foggy Mountain Breakdown*. Mercury.

Flippo, Chet. 2023. "Dolly Parton." *Country Music Hall of Fame and Museum*, April 27. www.countrymusichalloffame.org/hall -of-fame/dolly-parton.

Franklin, Paul. "Bio." http://www.paul-franklin.com/bio.html.

Franscio, Don. 1977. "He's Alive." *Forgiven 1977. NewPax*. Johnny Cash. "He's Alive."

Gallea, Rpn. 1978. "Dolly Parton with a Horse During an after Party Studio 54." https://www.gettyimages.ca/detail/news -photo/dolly-parton-with-a-horse-during-an-after-party-at -studio-news-photo/90879340?adppopup=true.

Garcia, Greta. 2023. "Dolly Parton and Carl Dean's Relationship Timeline." *Cosmopolitan*, November 10. https://www

.cosmopolitan.com/entertainment/celebs/a41980465/dolly
-parton-carl-thomas-dean-relationship-timeline/.

Genius. "The Moon and the Stars and Me." https://genius.com/
Dolly-parton-the-moon-the-stars-and-me-lyrics.

Genius. n.d. "Dolly Parton – He's Alive." *Genius*. https://genius
.com/Dolly-parton-hes-alive-lyrics.

Gentry Bobbi Fancy. 1970. *Capitol*.

Grammy.org. "Dolly Parton." https://www.grammy.com/artists/
dolly-parton/17205.

Griffiths, Dai. 2004. *Ok Computer*. New York: Continuum.

Hadden, Jeffery K. 1993. "The Rise and Fall of American
Televangelism." *The ANNALS of the American Academy of
Political and Social Science* 527, no. 1: 113–130. https://doi.org
/10.1177/0002716293527001009.

Hadden, Jeffery K., and Charles E. Swann. 1981. *Prime Time
Preachers: The Rising Power of Televangelism*. Middletown, CT:
Addison-Wesley.

Hammers, Lindsey L. 2017. "The Parton Paradox: A History of
Race and Gender in the Career of Dolly Parton." Master's
thesis, Georgia Southern University.

Harris, A. 2018. "An Update on Dolly Parton's (Formerly Dixie)
Stampede." *Slate Magazine*, April 12. https://slate.com/culture
/2018/04/a-visitor-describes-how-dolly-partons-stampede
-ditched-the-civil-war-theme.html.

Hee Haw. https://www.heehaw.com/#:~:text=Created%20by%20
Frank%20Peppiatt%20and,say%2C%20the%20rest%20is%20
history.

Hernandez, J. 2021b. "Dolly Invested Royalties from Whitney's 'I
Will Always Love You' in a Black Community." *NPR*, August
2. https://www.npr.org/2021/08/02/1023889920/dolly-parton
-invested-royalties-from-a-whitney-houston-cover-in-a-black
-communit.

The Hot Press Newsdesk. 2020. "Happy Birthday Dolly Parton: Revisiting her 2002 Interview with Hot Press." *Hotpress*, March 31. https://www.hotpress.com/culture/happy-birthday-dolly-parton-revisiting-2002-interview-hot-press-22764685.

Hughes, Charles. 2023. *Private Correspondence*. Memphis.

Jarell, Maya. n.d. "In the Mountains: Cherokee Culture Has a Rich History and Strong Influence in Southern Appalachia." https://www.lmc.edu/about/news-center/articles/2022/feature-article4.htm.

Jones, Hanna. 2023. "You Can Now Throw Your Own Dolly Parton Party Thanks to Walmart." *Country Living*, April 16.

Keefe, Susan Emley, and Thomas Plaut. 1996. "Susan Emley Keefe: Appalachia and Its People." In *People, Politics and Economic Life: Exploring Appalachia with Quantitative Methods*, 3–24. Appalachian State University. https://doi.org/10.2307/j.ctt1xp3m1b.5.

La Bruce, Bruce. "Notes on Camp and Anti Camp." http://www.natbrutarchive.com/essay-notes-on-campanti-camp-by-bruce-labruce.html.

Legman G. 1968/1975. *Rationale of the Dirty Joke: An Analysis of Sexual Humor*. New York: Grove Press.

Liebig, Lorie. 2022. "Dolly Parton Remembers Naomi Judd: Just Remember that I WIll Always Love You." May 3. https://tasteofcountry.com/naomi-judd-dead-dolly-parton-tribute/.

"Locust Ridge, Tennessee | Articles and Essays | Dolly Parton and the Roots of Country Music | Digital Collections | Library of Congress." n.d. The Library of Congress. https://www.loc.gov/collections/dolly-parton-and-the-roots-of-country-music/articles-and-essays/locust-ridge-tennessee/.

Martin, Douglas, and Lee Solters. "Razzle Dazzle PRess Agent, Dies at the Age of 89." https://www.nytimes.com/2009/05/22/theater/22solters.html

Matinez, Amanda. (2020). "Redneck Chic: Race and the Country Music Industry in the 1970s." *Journal of Popular Music Studies* 32, no. 2: 128– 43.

Mazor, Barry. 2009. *Meeting Jimmie Rodgers: How America's Original Roots Music Hero Changed the Pop Sounds of a Century.* London, New York: Oxford University Press.

McEntire, Reba. 1990. "Fancy." In *Rumor Has It*. MCA.

McEntire, Reba. 1990. *Rumor Has It*. MCA.

McEntire, Reba. 1990. "She Thinks His Name Was John." *Read My Mind*. MCA.

McNeil, W.K. 2005. *Encyclopedia of American Gospel Music.* Oxford, New York: Routledge, 54.

McMullen, Josh. 2015. "Old-Time Religion: Big Tent Revivalism and the Crisis of Late Victorian Culture." In *Under the Big Top: Big Tent Revivalism and American Culture, 1885–1925.* New York; (Online edn, Oxford Academic, December 18, 2014). https://doi.org/10.1093/acprof:oso/9780199397860.003.0003, accessed January 22, 2024.

Melnick, Lynn. 2022. *I've Had to Think Up a Way to Survive on Trauma Persistence and Dolly Parton.* Austin: University of Texas Press. https://doi.org/10.7560/322673.

Miller, Stephen. 2015. *Smart Blonde: Dolly Parton.* Revised ed. London: Overlook Omnibus, 240.

Miller Karl, Hagstrom. 2010. *Segregating Sound: Inventing Folk and Pop Music in the Age of Jim Crow.* Durham, NC: Duke University Press, 40.

Morris, Mitchell. 2013. *The Persistence of Sentiment: Display and Feeling in Popular Music of the 1970's.* Berkeley, CA: University of California Press.

Molanphy, Chris. 2020. "Country Was in a Chart Slump Until Garth Brooks Turned It into Arena-Size Spectacle." *Slate Magazine*, November 16. https://slate.com/podcasts/hit

-parade/2020/11/garth-brooks-rebooted-country-in-the-90s
-dominating-the-charts.

Morissey, Egan Tracie. 2024. "Dolly Parton's Boobs and Arms Are
Covered with Tattoos." *Jezebel*, May 9. https://jezebel.com/dolly
-partons-boobs-and-arms-are-covered-in-secret-tatt-1574168202.

NAMM, Oral History. Fred Vail. 2019. October 21. https://www
.namm.org/library/oral-history/fred-vail.

Newcomb, Horace. 1979. "Appalachia on Television: Region as
Symbol in American Popular Culture." *Appalachian Journal* 7,
no. 1/2: 155–164. http://www.jstor.org/stable/40932731.

Parton, Dolly. 1966. *Dumb Blonde*. Monument: RCA.

Parton, Dolly. 1973. *My Tennessee Mountain Home*. Victor: RCA.

Parton, Dolly. 1977a. "Me and Little Andy." In *Here You Come
Again*. Nashville: RCA.

Parton, Dolly. 1977b. "Applejack." In *New Harvest, First Gathering*.
Nashville: RCA.

Parton, Dolly. 1987. *Rainbow*. Columbia.

Parton, Dolly. 1989. *White Limozeen*. Columbia.

Parton, Dolly. 1999. *Grass is Blue*. Sugar Hill.

Parton, Dolly. 1994. *Dolly: My Life and Other Unfinished Business*.
1st ed. New York: HarperCollins.

Parton, Dolly, and Robert K. Oermann. 2020. *Dolly Parton:
Songteller My Life in Lyrics*. San Francisco: Chronicle Books.

Parton, Dolly, and Randy Schmidt. 2017. *Dolly on Dolly: Interviews
and Encounters*. Chicago, IL: Chicago Review Press.

The Parton Family. 1968. *In the Garden*. Nashville: Inspiration
Records.

Parton, Stella. 2011. *Tell It Sister, Tell It*. Attic Entertainment.

Paulson, Dave. 2015. "Dolly Parton Remembers Writing I Will
Always Love You." *Tennessean*, December 26.

Ragussis, Michael. 1993. "Writing Nationalist History: England,
the Conversion of the Jews, and Ivanhoe." *ELH* 60, no. 1:
181–215. http://www.jstor.org/stable/2873312.

Rayna, Green, Randolph Vance, and Frank A. Hoffmann. 1976. *Pissing in the Snow and Other Ozark Folktales*. Urbana: University of Illinois Press.

REO Speedwagon. 1978. "Time for Me to Fly You Can Tune a Piano but You Can't Tune a Fish." *Epic*.

Robertson, Pamela. 1999. "Mae West's Maids: Race, 'Authenticity, and the Discourse of Camp.'" In *Camp: Queer Aesthetics and the Performing Subject: A Reader*, edited by Fabio Cleto, 393–408. Edinburgh: Edinburgh University Press, 1999. http://www.jstor.org/stable/10.3366/j.ctvxcrp56.34.

Ross, Herbert, and Georges Delerue. 1989. *Steel Magnolias*.

Royster Francesca, T. 2022. *Black Country Music: Listening for Revolutions*. 1st ed. Austin: University of Texas Press. https://public.ebookcentral.proquest.com/choice/PublicFullRecord.aspx?p=7052672.

"Saturday Night Live s14e17 - Dolly Parton: SNL : Free Download, Borrow, and Streaming." 1989. *Internet Archive*, April 15. https://archive.org/details/saturday-night-live-s-14-e-17-dolly-parton.

Schumacher, Michael, and Denis Kitchen. 2013. *Al Capp: A Life to the Contrary First U.S.* New York: Bloomsbury.

Sharp, J.A. "150 Years of Severville." https://threefamilytrees.blogspot.com/2019/01/j-sharp-historian.html

Sisario, Ben. 2015. "Concord Music Group Buys Vangard and Sugar Hill." April 1. ttps://www.nytimes.com/2015/04/02/business/media/concord-music-group-buys-vanguard-and-sugar-hill.html.

Skaggs, Ricky. 1984. "Country Boy." *Country Boy. Epic.*

Smarsh, Sarah. 2023. *She Come By It Natural*. New York: Scribner.

Smith, Bessie. 1927. *Lock and Key Blues*.

Smithers, George. 2015. "Why Do So Many Americans Believe That They Have Cherokee Blood." *Slate*, October 5. https://

slate.com/news-and-politics/2015/10/cherokee-blood-why
-do-so-many-americans-believe-they-have-cherokee-ancestry
.html.

Sontag, S. 1964. *Notes on Camp*. New York, London: Penguin
Classics.

Staley, Karen. https://www.karenstaley.com.

Tewksbury, Joan. 1981. "Wild Texas Wind." *NBC*.

"The l Country Cast." 2022. October 25.

The Dolly Parton Discography. n.d. "The Dolly Parton
Discography." https://www.dollydiscography.com/.

The Today Show. 2013. February 1. https://www.today.com/video
/dolly-parton-reveals-why-she-s-hesitant-to-receive-medal-of
-freedom-100365893585.

"The Tonight Show Hosted by Johnny Carson." November 1989,
December 1990, and May 1991. Tapes in the collection of the
Pauley Center.

The Tonight Show Starring Jimmy Fallon. 2018. "Dolly Parton's
Husband Wants a Threesome with Jennifer Aniston." [Video].
*YouTube*, December 1. https://www.youtube.com/watch?v
=1PKEZ-BJX6s.

Thomas, Irma. 2014. "Fancy." *The Lost Cotillion Records*. Org
Records.

Thompson, Joey. 2023. *Private Correspondence*.

Vance, Randolph, and G Legman. 1992. *Unprintable Ozark
Folksongs and Folklore*. Fayetteville: University of Arkansas Press.

Various Artists. "Jesus People Music 1 and 2. Org Records."

Wachtell, C. 2012b. *The Author of the Civil War*, July 9. https://
archive.nytimes.com/opinionator.blogs.nytimes.com/2012/07
/06/the-author-of-the-civil-war/.

Walters, Barbara. 1977. "ABC News Interview with Dolly Parton."
December 6. https://abcnews.go.com/Entertainment/video/
road-dolly-parton-1977-66760052.

Weisbard, E. 2014. *Top 40 Democracy: The Rival Mainstreams of American Music*. Chicago: University of Chicago Press.

Whitburn, Joel. 2008. *Hot Country Songs 1944 to 2008*. Wauwatosa, Wisconsin: Record Research, Inc, 89.

Wilson, Carl. 2014. *Let's Talk About Love: Why Other People Have Such Bad Taste*. New and Expanded ed. New York: Bloomsbury, 153.

WYNC. 2015. "Dolly Parton's America." *Sad Ass Songs*, October 16.

Yahoo Is Part of the Yahoo Family of Brands. n.d. https://ca.news .yahoo.com/dolly-parton-sister-tweets-racist-185604396.html ?guccounter=1&guce_referrer=aHR0cHM6Ly93d3cuZ29vZ2x lLmNvbS8&guce_referrer_sig=AQAAAEfI-G16fSUIec8xhG70 2yHGgLjqVKmGzydhfULXUcoZNlRNRwjgVgOQgVb0yRtQ ZsXyX8Bo_5_YZ3Zt4kWG22mcQebZP0wIs6VrD6O8CA42sw 4F2ruDt9aPqVsUkdibBDdS2WuQLaMSSLV7rYcpLS513A VMdGQXQAV-nzx4ME_X https://www.ziprecruiter.com/Salaries/Dollywood-Salary.

Zaleski, Annie. 2021. *Rio*. New York: Bloomsbury Academic.

Zucchino, David. "At Randy Parton Theatre, Show Goes on without 'Star.'" *LA Times*, Septmber 17, 2007. https://www .latimes.com/news/la-na-parton17dec17-story.html.

# Also Available in the Series

ALSO AVAILABLE IN THE SERIES

# ALSO AVAILABLE IN THE SERIES